the *Lord* *saves me*

40 CHRIST-CENTERED FAMILY DEVOTIONS FROM THE PSALMS

IAIN M. DUGUID

PUBLISHING
P.O. BOX 817 • PHILLIPSBURG • NEW JERSEY 08865-0817

P&R Publishing offers special discount rates for bulk orders and ministry purchases. To inquire about a special rate, please write to us at sales@prpbooks.com.

Unless otherwise indicated, Scripture translations are the author's own.

A Scripture quotation from the New Testament uses the ESV's alternate, footnoted translation of *adelphoi* ("brothers and sisters").

Cover design by Jelena Mirkovic

Printed in the United States of America

Library of Congress Cataloging-in-Publication Data

Names: Duguid, Iain M., author.
Title: The Lord saves me : 40 Christ-centered family devotions from the Psalms / Iain M. Duguid.
Description: Phillipsburg : P&R Publishing, [2026] | Summary: "Show your children that the Psalms reflect their own experiences-and, more importantly, Jesus's life, death, and resurrection. Child-friendly translations of select psalms accompany gospel-centered devotional readings and prayers"-- Provided by publisher.
Identifiers: LCCN 2024051267 | ISBN 9798887790930 (hardcover) | ISBN 9798887790947 (epub)
Subjects: LCSH: Bible. Psalms--Devotional literature. | Devotional exercises. | Christian life--Reformed Presbyterian authors.
Classification: LCC BS1430.54 .D84 2025 | DDC 242/.5--dc23/eng/20241214
LC record available at https://lccn.loc.gov/2024051267

Contents

A Word to Readers

The psalms are the songs that God's Old Testament people sang in the temple in Jerusalem. They sang them as they waited for their Messiah to come—the one we know as Jesus. King David wrote many of these songs. Others were written by Moses, Solomon, and temple musicians such as Asaph and the sons of Korah. After the people of Israel were carried off to be slaves in Babylon, they collected the psalms into a book. They knew they needed to sing these songs so they could remember God's promises to them. *As you read the psalms in this book, look for God's good promises.*

Some of the psalms are celebratory and rejoicing songs that praise God for who he is. Others are songs of lament and mourning that ask God for help. Still others give thanks to God for rescuing his people. Some are instructional psalms that teach us how we should live. *As you read the psalms in this book, think about what kind of psalm each one is.*

Since King David wrote many of the psalms, they often give us the point of view of the king of Israel. We often read the psalms as if they are from *our* point of view. That isn't wrong, because David was one of God's sheep, just as we are. But sometimes we can understand the psalms better when we remember that a king is speaking. Plus, reading them this way reminds us that the psalms also point us forward to King David's greater son, Jesus. *As you read the psalms in this book, look for the presence of the king in the psalm.*

Jesus himself grew up singing the psalms. He tells us that the psalms speak about him. They tell us about his life and his suffering and about the glorious things that happened afterward (see Luke 24:44). After Jesus rose from the dead, his disciples often used the psalms to explain who he was and what he had come to earth to do. So it is important for us and our children to know not only the stories of the Old Testament but the psalms as well. Yes, the book of Psalms is a mirror that reflects back our own feelings of joy and sadness, but we must also learn to see how it shows us the sufferings of Jesus and the glories that are yet to come.

We can see Jesus in the psalms in a few simple ways. To begin with, we can remember that we are singing these psalms beside him. Jesus has felt the same joys, fears, and sorrows that we have—yet without sharing our sin. On his happiest days, Jesus always gave thanks perfectly to God. On his bad days, he always ran to God and made him his safe hiding place.

We can also think about Jesus singing these psalms when we can't. Some psalms show us things that happened to Jesus that are far harder and more painful than anything our heavenly Father will ever ask of us. Jesus is not only our friend in our sufferings but also our Savior who suffered in our place to rescue us.

We can also think of Jesus singing these psalms now, in the glory of heaven, as he looks forward to coming back to earth. We will not be sad and hurt forever. Some psalms show us the amazing party that will light up this sad world when everyone finally bows down to King Jesus. *As you read the psalms in this book, look for Jesus in every one.*

Words, People, and Places to Know

Ark of the covenant. A special box that reminded God's people that he was with them. In a way, it was the footstool of God's throne. It was the closest God's people could get to seeing *any* of his throne.

Babylon. One of Israel's biggest enemies, long ago. They captured Jerusalem because of Israel's sin and took most of the people away to be their slaves. But the Lord brought his people back to Jerusalem because he made a promise—and God can always be counted on to keep his promises.

Children of Adam. Human beings, who all come from the family that Adam and Eve started way back at the beginning. The children of Adam are the same kind of people (with all the same problems) that Adam was, because we all sin like he did.

Euphrates River. A big river in the land where Israel's enemies Assyria and Babylon lived. When Psalm 72:8 talks about how God's reign stretches from that river to the ends of the earth, that means that he rules over everyone.

God's name. God's name stands for, and tells us about, his character. His name is not only *the Lord* but everything that goes with that (see Exodus 34:6–7).

Holy. Set away from other things, on its own, and treated as special. God is holy, and so his people must be holy too. That means we must stay away from sin, keep all his rules, and follow his commands.

Israel. God's people, whom he rescued when they were slaves in Egypt and brought into the promised land–the land he had said he would give them.

Jacob. Abraham's grandson. Jacob was the father of twelve sons, who became the twelve tribes of Israel. In fact, God called *Jacob* "Israel," and the whole nation of God's people got its name from him.

Lord of Armies. Another way to say this is "the Lord of Hosts." This is a name for the Lord that reminds us that he is in charge of the strongest soldiers. In fact, armies (or "hosts") of *angels* serve and fight for him. They do whatever he tells them to.

Messiah. This word means "the Anointed One." In the time of Israel, kings and priests would be *anointed* when sweet-smelling oil was poured on their heads. This was a way of showing that they'd been specially blessed by God. They were signs, showing us that someday the true King and Priest, Jesus, would come and give us all God's blessings.

Mount Zion. The place where Solomon built the temple in the city of Jerusalem, high up on a mountain. Also known as "the Lord's mountain."

PSALM 1

[1] We should want to be the person
  who doesn't listen to bad people,
or go along with those who do wrong,
  or sit down with those who make fun of God.
[2] Instead, he loves to read God's Word
  and whispers it to himself all the time.
[3] He's like a tree
  that has been planted next to a stream:
Its leaves are always green,
  and every year it has lots of fruit.
Everything he does goes well.

[4] Bad people aren't like that.
  They are like straw blown away by the wind.
[5] They will not do well when God punishes those who
    do wrong,
nor will they be invited when God gathers good people
    to celebrate with him.

[6] This is because the Lord watches over the paths that
    good people take,
but the path bad people choose leads to disaster.

DAY 1

Like a Tree

Do you know someone who always seems happy? Maybe they always do well in school or win every game they play. Do you ever wish you could be more like that person?

Some people break the rules and aren't nice. They say bad things and like being mean. Do you ever wish you could be like *them*?

The psalm we just read, Psalm 1, tells us about the best kind of person to be: someone who stays away from bad people and doesn't listen to them . . . and who loves God's Word and thinks about it all the time. Is that what you do? I know *I* often don't love to read the Bible as I should, and I sometimes like to join bad people when they're saying bad things.

The writer of Psalm 1 tells us that the person who loves God will do well in everything they do. They will be like a tree that is planted close to the water. The water keeps the tree strong and healthy. We should all want to be like that!

The psalm also tells us about bad people. Yes, they sometimes seem to have fun, but the good things they have last for only a little while. Soon they will blow away like dry straw. This is because the Lord watches over good people, and he punishes bad people. Did you know that?

But aren't we *all* bad people, deep down inside? Even though we love Jesus, we still have mean hearts. We *all*—even moms and dads—do, and say, and think things that we shouldn't. Sometimes we don't want to listen to the Bible, or sit still in church, or pray. Sometimes we don't want to share our toys or be kind. We often do what *we* want to do—not what God tells us to. Do you ever act like that? I do.

Only one person in all of history has always been like the good person in this psalm. That person is Jesus. Jesus obeyed God the whole time he lived on earth. He always wanted to pray and to read God's Word, and he loved his parents and everyone around him. He never made fun of anyone or treated anyone badly.

But do you know what happened to Jesus? He died on a cross. God punished Jesus just like this psalm says he punishes bad people.

Do you know why Jesus was punished, even though he was God's perfect Son? It's because he took our place. At the cross, Jesus took the punishment we deserved for the bad things we do: He got in trouble instead of us, so that we could receive the prize he won for obeying perfectly. What is that prize? A happy life with God forever.

This is wonderful good news. If you believe in Jesus, then other people should want to be more like *you*! *Everyone* should want to be safe in Jesus and to have his goodness as their own. Let's give thanks to God for being so kind to bad people like us.

Dear heavenly Father, none of us are good people. Even though we love you, we still have mean and sinful hearts, like the bad people the psalm tells us to stay away from. Please forgive us, Lord. Thank you that Jesus came to rescue us by living a perfect life in our place. Help us love him and love your Word, the Bible, more and more. Help us want to do what is right. Thank you that, because of Jesus, you always watch over our steps and will never leave us alone, even when we disobey you. In Jesus's name, amen.

PSALM 2

¹ Why do nations get angry
  and people whisper together, even if it's useless?
² The rulers of the world come together to make plans
  against the Lord and his Chosen One:
³ They say, "Let's get rid of the ropes
  he has tied us up with!"

⁴ The Lord in heaven chuckles
  and laughs at their tantrums;
⁵ then he speaks to them in anger,
  and they are afraid of his fury.
⁶ He says, "I have placed my king on a throne on Mount
  Zion, where my holy temple is."

⁷ The Chosen One, the Messiah, says,
  "I'll tell people what the Lord said:

The Lord told everyone that I'm his Son
and he's my Father!
8 The Lord said, 'Ask me for the nations
and I'll give them to you as a present.
9 You'll break them with an iron bar,
shattering them into tiny pieces.'"

10 Be careful, kings!
Pay attention, judges of the earth!
11 Serve the Lord with fear
and be happy even though you are shaking!
12 Welcome the Son as your king,
or he may be angry and destroy you.
Running to hide in him is a good idea;
he'll soon be angry at those who don't.

DAY 2

Be Careful, Kings!

We live in a messed-up world. Bad people join together to fight against God, but this psalm tells us they can never win. In fact, God thinks their plans are funny. It's as if a baby wanted to fight somebody! People all over the world may kick and scream, but they will never get rid of God's rules. They just make life hard and sad for all of us.

Do *you* ever want to fight against God's rules?

The Lord is angry with those who try to fight against him or hurt his people. He's especially angry when anyone plans to fight or hurt his Chosen One. God has promised to protect his Chosen One from anyone who fights him, just like a good father protects his children from bullies.

The people who read this psalm in Old Testament times knew it was talking about King David.* David was God's chosen king of Israel. But this psalm was also telling them about David's very, *very* great-great-great-grandson. Do you know who that is?

Jesus is God's ultimate Chosen One. He is both the Son of David and the Son of God. God has put him in charge of the whole world. He runs everything perfectly.

* See 2 Samuel 7 for the whole story.

Even though Jesus is so good, we *all* start out as his enemies. Like the bad people in our psalm, we want to break free from him. We don't like his rules. We don't want to listen to him or obey. God is right to be angry when we fight against him.

This psalm tells us to stop fighting. Fighting is useless! God gives us the chance to welcome Jesus as his chosen, perfect king. He tells us to trust in Jesus and run to hide in him. He will keep us safe, and he will give us his goodness and make us good too.

Bad people can't win against Jesus, but one time it looked as though they had. Long ago, they nailed him to a cross. They put a sign above his head that said, "This is the King of the Jews." They thought that by killing him, they could get their own way. But when Jesus rose back to life again, the rest of this psalm came true: He became the strongest king forever.

Now people from all over the world are doing what this psalm tells us to do. God is saving people from every country on earth. People all over the world are bowing down to Jesus, the chosen king who rules forever. We can join them. When we bow down to Jesus, he becomes a safe hiding place and strong castle for us, just as the psalm says he will.

Heavenly Father, we often act like the people all over the world who fight against you: We want everything to go our own way. We don't listen to your loving rules or to our parents. We get angry when anyone tries to stop us from doing what we want to do. Please forgive us, Lord. Help us want to love and obey Jesus every day and find our safe hiding place in him. Thank you that he obeyed perfectly and died on the cross to make us into people who *can* love and obey him instead of fighting him. Thank you that now we are your children as well. Please help people from every country to worship him, love him, and want to obey him. Thank you for all the people in the world, including all the people we know, who do trust in him. We pray in Jesus's name, amen.

PSALM 3

A psalm by David, when he was running
away from Absalom, his son

[1] Lord, I have so many enemies!

So many people are ganging up on me

[2] and saying, "God won't save him."

[3] But you're my shield, Lord;

you're the one whose opinion really counts,

and you still see me as your friend.

[4] I called out to the Lord

and he answered me from the temple.

[5] I lay down and fell asleep;

I woke up because the Lord was protecting me.

[6] I'm not afraid of the millions of people

who are attacking me on all sides.

[7] Get up, Lord! Save me, God!

You always punch my enemies in the mouth;

you break the teeth of those who are bad.

[8] The Lord saves me;

your smile rests on your people!

DAY 3

The Lord Saves Me

Has someone ever really scared you? What did they do to make you so scared?

You've probably never been scared because someone wanted to kill you, have you? But one time King David's own son, Absalom, tried to kill him and be king in his place. Can you imagine how sad and scared David felt?

David had to run away from home. He ran far away to hide from Absalom and his soldiers. Could *you* sleep if you knew a big army might be sneaking up on you? David tells us in this psalm that he slept great! He knew God was with him. He knew God would be his shield to keep him safe. He knew God would hear him call for help and answer his prayers. That's why David wasn't afraid.

Are you ever afraid? It's normal to feel scared when bad things happen. But our powerful God loves us. He protects us because he is our perfect Father. Even scary things that hurt us are under his control. He will always make sure that even the bad, scary things that happen end up being good for us.

David was certain that this was true, but we can be even *more* certain. Why? Because we know the story of Jesus. That story shows exactly how God makes bad things turn out for good.

Jesus had enemies, just like David's enemies in this psalm. We might expect God to punch Jesus's enemies in the face, but that's not what happened. To rescue us from our sins, God let the people who hated Jesus punch *him* in the face and treat him like he was God's enemy.

Those bad people were sure that God wouldn't save Jesus. But God did! He raised Jesus from the dead and put him in charge of his kingdom.

God saved David, and he saved Jesus, and he saves people like us too, even though we don't deserve it at all! Isn't that wonderful? Because Jesus took our punishment for us, we are now God's friends. God now smiles on us with love and joy, and we know he will always be our shield. He will always protect us. We don't need to be scared anymore!

Lord God, thank you that you always hear our prayers, for Jesus's sake, and always protect us. Help us remember your strength and love so we can sleep without fear when life is scary. Please protect us from those who want to hurt us, and remind us that we are always safe in you. We ask you to stop bullies from being able to hurt your people, Lord, and to remind us always to thank you for making us your children when we trust in Jesus. Amen.

PSALM 4

A psalm by David

[1] Answer me when I call, O God—the God who says I am
   right with you;
   when I was in a tight spot, you gave me room
   to breathe;
   be kind and listen to my prayer.

[2] How long will you strong people hate me and make
   fun of me?
   You love silly things and run after your fake gods.
[3] Remember, the Lord has chosen the faithful one to
   be his;
   the Lord will listen to me when I call to him.

[4] It's okay to feel angry, but don't sin when you're angry;
   when you are in bed, talk to yourself and calm down.
[5] Give the proper sacrifices to the Lord
   and trust in him.
[6] Many people ask, "Who will give us good things?"
   Lord, let us see your face smiling down on us.
[7] You make me happier than others,
   even when they have a lot of delicious food to eat.
[8] I will lie down and go to sleep peacefully,
   for only you, Lord, keep me safe.

DAY 4

The Lord Will Listen to Me

Can you remember a time when your life felt really hard? Did you ask God to help you?

Many people completely forget about God when they are in a tight spot. They know they need *something* or *some-one* to help them, but they trust the wrong things. Today's psalm talks about people who turn to fake gods—idols—that they worship and hope will keep them safe. They think these idols will give them what they want.

When he wrote this psalm, King David and his people were in a tight spot. Some people said that idols could get them out of their trouble. They were wrong.

David wrote his psalm to those people. They were scared. David tells them that he is not. Even when he is in danger, he knows that God will listen to him, keep him safe, and give him everything he needs.

Are you like David when things are going wrong? I'm often more like David's people. It's easy for me to be angry and scared, especially at night. I toss and turn and worry. I forget that God watches over everyone who trusts in Jesus. His face smiles down at them and shines with love.

Why does God smile down at us? Is it because we are so good? Actually, no one can be right or loyal enough to become one of God's people on their own. Only Jesus can make us faithful and right with God, because he is the *Most Faithful One*. He was so faithful that he went all the way to the cross. He faced the worst and hardest thing anyone ever suffered: The face of God the Father, which had always shone down on him, turned away from him and left him alone in the dark.

Now Jesus doesn't just give us good *things*, like the people in this psalm wanted. No, he actually gives us his own goodness—the kind of goodness the Father loves. This is why God smiles at us all the time. It's why we can lie down and sleep instead of tossing and turning, no matter how hard life is: God loves us, for Jesus's sake, and always holds us in his strong arms. Because he turned his face away from Jesus on the cross, he will never turn his face away from *us* or leave us alone.

Heavenly Father, when we think you have forgotten us, show us that you still hear our prayers. When we are scared, worried, or angry, talk to our hearts and help us calm down and sleep in peace. Remind us that because of Jesus, we are never alone. He loves us and will never leave us. Help us not to trust in fake gods but to place our trust only in you. Amen.

PSALM 8

A psalm by David

[1] O Lord, our Master,

you are very famous all over the world;
your brightness shines out higher than the heavens!
[2] You have used the praise of even children and infants
to build a strong castle—
one that keeps out dangerous people who want to
hurt us.
[3] When I look up at your heavens, which your fingers
made,
the moon and the stars that you put in place,
[4] what is a human person that you would notice him,
or a son of Adam that you should bother to take
care of him?
[5] You made him a little lower than the angels,
and you gave him a beautiful and shiny crown!
[6] You made him the ruler over everything you made:
[7] All the sheep and cows,
the wild animals,
[8] the birds of the sky and the fish of the sea
—everything that swims in the sea.
[9] O Lord, our Master,

you are very famous all over the world.

DAY 5

You Are Very Famous All over the World

David wrote this psalm, Psalm 8, to say how happy he was. Why was he happy? Because God, who is so important and famous, cares about us. He pays attention to us even though we are so much less important and powerful than him.

Our God is so amazing. He put the moon and the stars in their faraway places. He made all kinds of different animals. He has done great things that everyone can see . . . but he still takes the time to look after us. Imagine that!

David was also happy because God gave *us* this world he made. Did you know that God made all the amazing animals so that you can enjoy them—and also look after them? We often feel small and weak, but God has given us a special job in his world. We are his workers, and he is our Master. We are very important to the Lord!

But the amazing world that God made has changed. Do you remember what Adam and Eve did? Instead of ruling perfectly over the world that God had made, they disobeyed him. And because they disobeyed him and sinned, this world God made for us is no longer a safe place. Now it is filled with many dangers and many people who can hurt us.

But God fixed this problem for us. He sent Jesus into our dangerous world as a baby. When Jesus grew up and died on the cross many years later, he didn't just save and protect disobedient children of Adam, like us—no, he also made a way for his whole world to be saved one day. All the animals and birds and fish that this psalm talks about will be made new and perfect again.

We can look forward to living with Jesus in a wonderful new world where there are no enemies or dangers. And while we wait for that day, we should make this amazing and famous God even *more* famous by shouting happily about his love everywhere we go!

Creator God, thank you for the wonderful job you gave to people when you first made us: You placed us at the very top of your world so that we could take care of it. Forgive us for disobeying you like Adam and wandering away from you. We have all done what we wanted to do rather than serving you and doing our special job the right way. Thank you for rescuing us and making a way for even the earth and moon and stars to be made beautiful and new again. We love you, and we want your power and kindness to be celebrated and made even more famous by everyone around the world. Amen.

PSALM 11

A psalm by David

[1] In the Lord, I am safe.
How can you say to me,
    "Fly away like a bird from your mountain.
[2] Look, the bad people have bent their bow
    and strung their arrow
    to shoot from the shadows at good people.
[3] When the foundations are broken down,
    what can a good person do?"

[4] The Lord is in his holy temple;
    his throne is in heaven.
    His eyes see everything; he studies the children
    of Adam.
[5] The Lord studies both good and bad people;
    he hates anyone who loves violence.
[6] He will rain fire down on bad people;
    he will pay them back with a burning hot wind.

[7] For the Lord is good,
so he loves it when people do good;
    those who do what is right will see his smiling face.

The Lord Is Good

Think about the last time you felt scared. What did you do?

Psalm 11 gives us two choices we can make any time we are scared: a good choice and a bad choice. David's friends wanted him to make the bad choice. When he was in danger, they told him, "Run away! Save yourself! There is nothing you can do!"

But David didn't follow their advice. He made the right choice. He chose to hide in the Lord instead.

David knew that God sits on his throne in heaven. And from that throne, God watches everything that happens on the earth. Do you think he misses anything? No, he sees *all* the bad things that people do every day. He saw Adam and Eve's first sin, and he punished them. When he decides it's time, he will punish everyone for *all* their sins. Only those who do what is right will see God's smiling face in heaven.

But none of us do what is right, do we? Like Adam, we all have sinned. We make bad choices all the time. If God watches us, he'll see that we are too bad to be treated like good people. We deserve to be punished with fire and burning hot wind, like the bad people in this psalm.

This is scary, isn't it? The good news is that Jesus has rescued us from that punishment. Jesus came to be the kind of good person that we can't be. For his whole life, he made perfect choices all the time. He never did anything wrong. God tested him and saw that his thoughts, words, and actions were always perfect.

Then Jesus made a trade. He took the punishment for all the bad things that we have done. And he gave us his goodness so that God can smile on us forever.

Because Jesus did that for us, you and I can find a safe hiding place in the Lord. What good and wonderful news!

Lord God, you sit on your throne in heaven and rule over the whole earth. Thank you for being perfectly good and holy and for punishing all those who enjoy doing what is wrong. Thank you that Jesus lived a perfect life and made a trade so that we could be treated like we lived his perfect life instead. Help us do what we can to do good. Help us trust that you will welcome us into heaven to see your smiling face when we die, for Jesus's sake. You are our forever safe hiding place from all dangers. Amen.

PSALM 14

A psalm by David

¹ The fool says in his heart, "God isn't real!"
People like that have twisted thoughts and do
terrible things.
There isn't anyone on earth who does what is good.

² The Lord stares down from heaven on the children
of Adam
to see if there is anyone who understands and
looks for God.
³ Everyone has gone offtrack; they have all become
rotten inside;
there isn't anyone who does what is good,
not even one.

⁴ Don't all these bad people understand,
    who swallow up my people like they gulp down
        their food
    and never call upon the Lord?

⁵ Right where they are, they will be scared to death,
    for God is with those who do what is right.
⁶ You may try to mess up the plans of the weak person,
    but the Lord is his safe hiding place.

⁷ I wish Israel's rescue would come from Mount Zion!
    When the Lord sorts out the problems of his people,
    Jacob will be happy, and Israel will shout for joy!

DAY 7

There Isn't Anyone Who Does What Is Good

Are you a fool? Do you ever act in ways that don't make sense?

We all like to think we are smart, not silly like a fool. But people who think God isn't real are making a big, silly, awful mistake. If they think God isn't real, they don't think about what God wants them to do. If they don't think about what God wants them to do, they think they can do whatever *they* want. That might sound good at first . . . but when we do whatever we want, we always end up hurting others—and ourselves too. The things *we* want to do are often foolish and not good at all.

This is why, in the psalm we just read, David says that no one does any good. We are all children of Adam, the first human being. As his children, we all do bad things just like he did. In fact, we do *terrible* things. Even our thoughts get twisted and wrong. We are rotten on the inside.

David has seen people try to ruin things for anyone who is weaker than they are. He has even seen people act like they want to swallow up anyone who tries to follow God! Maybe you have seen people like that too.

It's silly to say God isn't real. He *is* real, and one day he will come and judge everyone. He will punish bad people for all their bad thoughts, words, and deeds. He will even punish bad people for all the nice things they did just to make themselves *look* good.

When God comes to punish bad people, they will be scared to death. They will see how wrong they were to do whatever they wanted. They will see how silly it was to say God isn't real.

But remember what we learned on other days. Jesus has given us *his* goodness. Because of Jesus, God sees us as his own precious children instead of as foolish children of Adam. That means that when God comes to punish bad people, we don't have to be scared of him. He is our safe hiding place. We will be happy and will sing about how he has rescued us with his wonderful grace.

Heavenly Father, please help us not to be fools. Teach us to think of you every day and remember that you are our kind Maker and our safe hiding place. Help us remember that your wise rules are here to guide us, and to *protect* us from doing whatever we want. Thank you that Jesus has saved us so we don't need to be scared to death by your anger. Thank you that he will be our safe hiding place on the day when you judge everyone. If we belong to him, no one can say we are guilty, no matter what terrible things we've thought and done. Help us rejoice and be happy over that good news. Amen.

PSALM 19

A psalm by David

¹ The heavens show us God's glory,
   and the sky shouts aloud the work of his hands.
² Every day speaks to us,
   while every night teaches us something.
³ The skies don't talk or make a sound,
⁴ but their lesson goes throughout the world,
   their message to the ends of the earth.
The sun has set up his tent in the heavens:
   ⁵ He comes out like a bridegroom leaving his bedroom;
like a champion athlete, he is excited to run his race
   each day.
⁶ The sun rises at one end of the heavens
   and goes round to the other;
   nothing is hidden from its heat.

⁷ The Lord's teaching is perfect,
   helping people live a full life;
the Lord's words can be counted on,
   making children wise;
⁸ the Lord's instructions are right,
   making hearts happy;
the Lord's commandments are pure,
   lighting up people's eyes.

9 Fearing the Lord is healthy,
    forever and ever;
the Lord's decisions are trustworthy
    and completely right.
10 They are better than gold—
    even lots of the very best gold;
they are sweeter than honey—
    even honey straight from the beehive.
11 By them, God's servants know what to do,
    and there are great rewards for those who keep
        them.

12 Who can see their own mistakes?
    Clean me from my hidden sins.
13 Protect your servant from sinning boldly;
    don't let such awful sins rule over me.
Then I will be without fault,
    washed clean from my selfish and self-centered
        attitude.
14 Let the words in my mouth and the thoughts in
        my heart
    make you happy,
    Lord, my Rock and my Rescuer.

The Lord's Teaching Is Perfect

Do you like following instructions? Most of us think that rules and instructions keep us from doing what we want. "Do this!" says a rule, but our hearts say, "Don't!"

When we read today's psalm, did you notice how David felt about God's instructions? He said they are good and right. He even said they are beautiful like gold and tasty like the sweetest honey. He seemed very happy about God's teaching, didn't he? Why do you think that is?

David gives us a clue. He says that the sun shouts God's glory by running through the sky like a racing champion or like a man rushing to get to his wedding. God gave the sun instructions to follow, and the sun *happily* obeys them. We were made the same way: When we follow God's intstructions and do what he created us to do, we shine out his glory!

The sun doesn't make any mistakes or wander away. We would have a big problem if it did. But *we* wander away from God's teaching all the time, don't we? We make mistakes. We disobey God. We hide our sins by doing them only when other people aren't watching. We pretend that the bad things we do aren't a big deal. Sometimes we even feel proud about not following God's instructions. We would disobey all the time, except God kindly holds us back and protects us from making only bad choices.

How can our words and our thoughts make our holy God happy? God must become our Rock and our Rescuer. He must save us from the bad things that happen when we ignore his instructions and don't follow them.

Can you guess how Jesus is like the sun? When he came to live on earth, he happily obeyed God and shone out his glory. For his whole life, he followed God's instructions perfectly. He never sinned in secret. He was never selfish or self-centered. And when we ask him to be our Rescuer, he washes us clean from our sins and gives us his perfect life as our own.

When we are washed clean, we can love his rules like Jesus did. We can see that the God who tells us "Do this!" is the same kind Father who sent his own Son to die on a cross to save us. When he tells us to do something, it is because he loves us so much. His rules are always for our good. That is one reason David says they are sweet!

They are sweet for another reason too. When we follow God's instructions, we are showing God that we love him. We are thanking him for loving us enough to send his Son to rescue us.

Heavenly Father, forgive us for disobeying your instructions instead of loving and obeying them. Help us look to our Rescuer, Jesus, to clean us from all our sins. Help us love the wisdom you show as our Father, and help us trust that your teaching is always good for us, even when it's hard for us to obey. We love you, Lord. Amen.

PSALM 22:1-8

A psalm by David

¹ My God, my God, why have you left me alone?
You are far away from saving me, despite my painful
  cries.
² My God, I call to you during the day, but you don't
  answer,
  and I call again at night, but I hear no reply.

³ You are the Holy One,
  surrounded by Israel's songs of praise.
⁴ Our parents trusted in you:
  They trusted, and you rescued them.
⁵ They cried out to you, and they escaped;
  they trusted in you, and you never let them down.

⁶ But I am only a worm, not a person,
  mocked and hated by everyone.
⁷ Everyone who sees me makes fun of me;
  they make fun of me and shake their heads at me.
⁸ They say, "He depended on the Lord: Let the Lord
  deliver him;
  let him rescue him if he likes him so much."

DAY 9

Why Have You Left Me Alone?

Does it surprise you that King David wrote a psalm about feeling let down by God, even though he was God's chosen one? Then maybe it would surprise you even more to know that *Jesus* also felt left alone by his Father. He knows exactly how it feels to think that God isn't listening or doesn't care.

How do we know that? We know that because, when Jesus was dying on the cross, he said the first line of this psalm. "My God, why have you left me alone?"

When David thought God had left him alone and wasn't answering him, he still called him "my God." He still cried out to God for help and depended on him. He still trusted God for everything, even though everyone around him told him that God had forgotten him. And Jesus did just the same. Even though he knew he was going to die, he still prayed that God would do whatever he wanted and what he thought was best.*

---

* "Father, if you are willing, remove this cup from me. Nevertheless, not my will, but yours, be done" (Luke 22:42 ESV).

When Jesus was on the cross, he felt *all* the badness of *all* his people's sins. This hurt him very much. It was so bad that, when God didn't stop it, Jesus felt like he had gone far away and left him alone. But he also knew that God would not let his pain stop until he had paid for every single wrong thing we have ever said and thought and done. Only then could Jesus say, "It is finished!"

On the cross, Jesus won the fight against sin to make us safe. "God is no longer angry at those who belong to Jesus."* Even if we sometimes feel like David did, as if God is far away, God will *never* stay far away from us. Nothing can keep him from answering us when we call to him for help. Nothing can keep him from loving us. God is happy with us because of Jesus, and he will certainly rescue us from all dangers.

> Beloved Father of Jesus, thank you for sending your Son to pay for all the wrong things we have done. Thank you for counting his pain as ours so that his victory over sin counts as ours as well. When we feel helpless and alone, help us believe that you are always with us. Teach us to trust in you when we are hurt and when people are mean to us. We know that you care about us, no matter what other people say. You are our God, and you always save your people. Amen.

* Romans 8:1.

PSALM 22:22-28

²² I will tell the members of my family how great you are;

 I will praise you with your people.

²³ You who fear the Lord, praise him;

 all you children of Jacob, tell everyone the great

 things he has done;

 all you children of Israel, be amazed by our God.

²⁴ For he has not ignored or made fun of

 the pains of people who are in difficulty;

he has not looked away when they most needed help—

 when they cried to him for help, he listened.

²⁵ Because you are with me, I will praise you when your

 people gather together;

 I will do what I promised in front of those who

 respect you.

²⁶ Those who are hungry will eat and have enough;

 those who long to be with the Lord will praise him.

 May these people live forever!

²⁷ The most distant places on earth will remember

 and turn to the Lord;

All families of nations

 will bow down before him,

²⁸ because the royal throne belongs to the Lord;

 he rules over the nations.

DAY 10

I Will Praise You

The last time we heard from King David, he felt very sad and alone. Doesn't he sound much happier today? Psalm 22 started "My God, my God, why have you left me alone?" but it ends with happy words of praise. When all David's people came together to worship God, he was excited to tell them how the Lord had rescued him from his problems.

God is amazing and does great things. He never makes fun of people who need help. Instead, he rescues them. This is why people from all over the world should praise and thank God together. Are you ready to join them and sing to him too? What can you praise God for today?

The New Testament tells us that Psalm 22 is about Jesus. Remember how alone he felt on the cross? That was not the end of his story. God always keeps his promises! He raised Jesus from the dead and brought him to stand right next to him in heaven. Do you know what Jesus is doing right now? He is leading a big celebration with everyone he has saved.*

---

* "[Jesus says], 'I will tell of [God's] name to my brothers and sisters; in the midst of the congregation I will sing your praise'" (Hebrews 2:11–12 ESV).

Because Jesus finished his work on earth perfectly, everyone who trusts in him becomes part of his own family. We are all, like him, the children of God the Father.* God takes care of everyone who is his.

Jesus died to rescue the children of Israel. But he also died to save families from every country on the earth. Do you know that many people all over the world, even in the most distant places, know and trust in Jesus? But a lot of people in the world *don't* trust in him yet. Many have never even heard of him. We should pray for people all over the world to hear and believe the good news about Jesus.

We can also *help* people hear that good news! Like David, and like the Lord Jesus, we should be so excited about God that we can't wait to tell other people about him. After all, our great God has done great things.

Mighty God, thank you that Jesus died to save us and has made us part of your family forever. Please let us join the praises that people sing around the world because of your kindness and goodness, and help us sing Jesus's praises as well. Please let other people around the world hear the good news—and send us people to speak to about you. Thank you, Lord. Amen.

* "To all who . . . believed in his name, he gave the right to become children of God" (John 1:12 ESV).

PSALM 23

A psalm by David

¹ The Lord is my shepherd; I am his sheep, so he makes
    sure I have whatever I need.
    ² He brings me to fields with lots of green grass
        where I can rest,
and he makes sure I have safe places to drink.
    ³ He builds up my strength;
he guides me along straight paths—
    and all for his glory.
⁴ Even when I go through dark and dangerous valleys,
    I will not be afraid of anything,
for you are with me.
    Your stick and your shepherd's crook
        make me feel safe.
⁵ You lay out a feast for me
    in front of my enemies;
you put sweet-smelling lotion on my head,
    and my cup is filled to the very top.
⁶ I know that your goodness and faithful love will
        hunt me down,
and I will live with you forever and ever.

DAY 11

The Lord Is My Shepherd

What do you think a sheep needs to be happy? Did you notice what this psalm told us?

Psalm 23 starts out by describing a good shepherd who loves his sheep very much. He takes good care of them. In the spring, he makes sure his sheep have plenty to eat and drink. When it gets hot and dry, and the only grass and water still left are hidden in the shade of dangerous rocks and cliffs, the good shepherd leads his flock there. He also watches over them the whole time to protect them from wild animals and other problems.

Did you notice who the shepherd is? God.

And who are the sheep? We are!

But is this whole psalm just about a shepherd and sheep? No, it starts telling its story in a different way partway through. It tells us that God will throw an amazing feast for us. He will welcome us into his royal palace, pour sweet-smelling lotion on our heads, and fill our plates and cups with the best food and drink. Our enemies will no longer be able to hurt us, because everyone will know that we are God's special friends and he will keep us safe. Best of all, we won't have to leave this party: We will get to feast with God forever!

God doesn't do all this for us because we're great people. He does it to show how great *he* is.

Did you notice some strange wording in this psalm? It said that God's goodness and love would hunt us down! But for that to be possible, God's *anger* hunted Jesus down. God was angry at our sin, but Jesus took that sin for us so that God would punish him instead.

That meant that God did not protect Jesus from his enemies, the way he now protects us. No, Jesus's enemies made fun of him and hurt him. Jesus didn't get to enjoy a wonderful time with God. He died on a cross instead, and God left him alone instead of helping him. Then, instead of resting in a safe, green place, Jesus was buried in a cold, dark grave. How hard that must have been! But he went through all those awful things because he loved us and wanted to save us.

Once Jesus paid for our sins, God made everything right. He raised Jesus from the dead. He made him the most famous and most loved person of all time. Jesus is happy again, and he is waiting to welcome us to his amazing feast!

Heavenly Father, thank you that Jesus let himself get hunted by your anger so that we wouldn't have to suffer for our sins. Thank you that Jesus has risen from the dead so that he can be with us all the time. Thank you that he will welcome us into your house forever, if we trust in you. Please help us to trust you when life is scary and to thank you on days when you give us everything we need. Take care of us, we pray, both now and forever. In Jesus's name, amen.

PSALM 24

A psalm by David

¹ The earth and all its creatures belong to the Lord;
   the world and everyone who lives in it are his.
² He built it on the seas
   and set it up firm on the rivers.

³ Who may go up the Lord's mountain?
   Who can stand in his holy temple?
⁴ The person who serves him with his hands and his
   heart,
   who hasn't given his heart to fake gods
   or broken his promises.
⁵ He will receive the Lord's smile
   and be counted as right by the God who saves us.
⁶ People like that are the kind of people who seek God,
   who want to meet with him—the way Jacob did!

[7] Gates, lift up your heads;

eternal doors, look up

and see that the glorious King is coming!

[8] Who is this glorious King?

He is the Lord, strong and mighty,

the Lord, mighty in battle!

[9] Gates, lift up your heads;

eternal doors, look up

and see that the glorious King is coming!

[10] Who is this glorious King?

He is the Lord of Armies;

he is the glorious King!

DAY 12

The Glorious King Is Coming!

In Psalm 24, David tells us three important things about God. First, our God is the *Creator*. He made everything in heaven and on earth, even the wild seas and the flooding rivers. Second, our God is a glorious *King*. As king, he fights battles to protect his kingdom, and he always wins. And third, our God is *holy*.

What does it mean for God to be holy? It means that not just anyone can meet with him. The only people who can meet him are people who love him more than they love anything else. They must love him so much that they keep their hearts and hands from doing anything wrong. Only people like that will be allowed to see him march into his city in heaven. I want to see that parade, don't you?

David says people who want to meet with God should be like Jacob. If you know the Bible's stories about Jacob, you might be surprised. Wasn't Jacob a thief and a liar? He was! Didn't he try to steal his brother's blessing, even though the Lord had already promised it to him?* Yes, he

---

* You can read the whole story in Genesis 25–28.

did! How could someone as bad as Jacob be good enough to appear before God?

Our mighty Lord of Armies made himself very small on the day Jesus came to earth. And Jesus's enemies led him in a parade, too—but it wasn't a parade back home to his city to celebrate him. It was a parade *away* from the city to kill him.

Jesus is the only person who always used his hands and heart to serve God. He always thought and did the right thing. He is the only person who has never loved anything or anyone more than God. He is the only person who ever decided to serve God perfectly—and then *did*. Yet when he went to the cross, Jesus was treated the same as if he were guilty of every one of our sins.

When we trust in Jesus, we get the reward that Jesus deserved. The God who saves us counts us as people who are right. Because Jesus gave us his perfectly clean heart, even bad people like Jacob—and like you and me—can come into that city in heaven and be welcomed into God's house. Now we can go up the Lord's mountain!

One day, the Lord, the glorious King, will come back to show that his kingdom belongs to him. It will be the greatest parade and celebration of all time. On that day, everyone will bow down before him as king. And all those who trust in him will enter his holy temple—because our holy, glorious, Creator King is also the God who saves us!

Lord God, you are the Creator of everything and the glorious King. Thank you for Jesus's clean hands and his sinless heart, which you give to bad people like us. Like Jacob, we do many wrong things, and it is only because of Jesus that we are able to pray to you at all. Please help us remember that Jesus is the glorious King who sits on his throne in heaven. Please help us look forward eagerly to the day when he will come back to celebrate his victory. Come soon, Lord Jesus. We can't wait to worship you in your holy temple! Amen.

PSALM 32:1-7

A psalm by David

¹ Happy is the person whose wrongs are forgiven
  and whose sin is buried by God.
² Happy is the person whom the Lord doesn't count
    as being guilty
  yet who doesn't pretend they have never done
  anything wrong.

³ When I kept quiet about my sin, I was dying inside:
  I groaned sadly all day long.
⁴ Day and night you punished me;
  I felt like a dried-up river in a summer drought.
⁵ Then I admitted what I had done wrong
  and stopped trying to hide it.
I said, "I'll say sorry for my sin to the Lord";
  you forgave the wrong I had done and took away
    my guilt.

⁶ Therefore, let all the faithful people
  pray to you while you are holding your arms open.
When the mighty waters flood,
  they cannot touch them.
⁷ You are my safe hiding place;
  you protect me from trouble;
  you surround me with songs that tell people about
    my deliverance.

You Are My Safe Hiding Place

Have you ever done something wrong and tried to cover it up? Maybe you broke something and then hid it so no one would know. Maybe you said something you shouldn't have and then tried to keep your brother or sister from telling your parents.

How did you feel when you tried to hide this bad thing you did? You probably felt guilty and afraid that someone would find out the truth. That's a sad way to try to live, isn't it? David says in our psalm that *he* tried to live this way, but hiding made him so unhappy that he felt like he was dying.

God knows we're always doing the wrong thing! We can't fool him, and we can't solve our problems without him. We need to tell him that we are sorry instead of hiding. Then, because he loves us, he will take away our sin *and* our guilt. We can be happy again.

Why does God forgive our sins? Only because God asked Jesus to pay for all of them and Jesus said yes. God took all the punishment that we deserved and piled it on Jesus instead. He took all the love and protection that Jesus deserved and gave it to us instead. That means that he now holds his arms open to us and loves us and protects us from trouble.

Because of Jesus, we can pray to our heavenly Father and can know that he'll listen to us. He hears us when we ask for help, and he'll be our safe hiding place when we're in trouble. Because of Jesus, we can sing songs and hymns when we celebrate how God has rescued us. He saved us from being punished for our sin. He even saved us from the power sin used to have over us. We really are happy people!

> Thank you, Lord, for being such a kind and forgiving God—a God we can run to whenever we have done something wrong. Thank you that your mercy is as wide and deep as the ocean. Thank you that, because of Jesus, we have a safe hiding place on the day when you will remember, and judge, everything we have done. Thank you for judging Jesus for our sins instead, so we will not be counted guilty. In Jesus's name, amen.

PSALM 33:12-22

¹² We should want to be the nation the Lord calls
  his own,
    the people he chose for himself.
¹³ The Lord gazes down from heaven
    and sees all Adam's children.
¹⁴ From his heavenly throne, he studies
    everyone who lives on earth.
¹⁵ He shapes their hearts
    and understands all their actions.

¹⁶ No king is saved by how big his army is;
    no soldier is protected by his great strength.
¹⁷ It is silly to think a warhorse could save you;
    its great power can't rescue anyone.
¹⁸ But the Lord watches over people who respect him,
    those who rely on his faithful love;
¹⁹ he saves them from death and keeps them alive
    when there isn't enough food.

²⁰ We depend on the Lord;
    he is our helper and our shield.
²¹ Our hearts rejoice in him;
    we trust in how holy he is because he is God.
²² May your faithful love rest on us, Lord,
    as we trust in you.

DAY 14

We Depend on the Lord

This psalm tells us there are two kinds of people: Adam's children and the people God chooses for himself. We all start out as Adam's children. Like Adam, we disobey God. And God is looking down from heaven to see these bad things we do.

But God also sees that we need help. So, before Jesus came to earth, God chose the people of Israel to be his people. Israel was a small, weak country. God chose to watch over it and protect the Israelites from their enemies. And so, any time they won a battle, it was silly for them to think they had won it by themselves. That's why this psalm says that Israel's kings and strong soldiers, and even the big, fierce horses they rode on, weren't what protected or saved them. It was God who rescued them!

God wanted to rescue even more people than just the people in Israel. He decided to choose people from every country and town to belong to him. So now, when we trust in God and depend on him and his Son Jesus, we become God's children too. God makes our hearts into *new* hearts and fills our lives with the good things he wants us to do.

We can have the same special relationship with him that his people in Israel had.

God watches over us and cares for us from his throne in heaven. He knows what we are thinking and why we do what we do. So when we have to deal with problems, it is silly for us to depend on our own cleverness and strength—as silly as it would have been for Israel to depend on its little army. We are not smart enough or strong enough to take care of things on our own! Instead, we can depend on God's strength and trust in him. After all, he is wise and holy and good because he is God. Because Jesus has rescued all the people God chose, God loves us always. We know he will never leave us on our own, because we are his beloved children.

Heavenly Father, we thank you that you have chosen us and called us your own people, just like Israel. Thank you that you love us and sent Jesus to save us, even though we are big sinners like Adam. Please forgive us for trusting our own strength and cleverness instead of you. We think that other people can save us from our problems, and so we forget to pray to you. Remind us that you will never abandon us, and teach us to trust in you always—even when we feel scared. Amen.

PSALM 46

A psalm by the Sons of Korah

¹ God is our safe hiding place and strength,
a helper who is right beside us in times of trouble.
² Therefore, we won't be afraid—even if the earth falls apart
and the mountains collapse into the depths of the seas;
³ even when the waves crash and foam
and the mountains shake under the sea's attacks.

⁴ There is a river whose streams make happy the city of God,
where the Most High lives.
⁵ God lives in that city, so nothing can shake it.
God will come to help it as soon as the morning comes.

6 Nations growl, kingdoms break in pieces,
  the earth itself falls apart when he raises his voice.
7 The Lord of Armies is with us;
  the God of Jacob is our strong castle.

8 Look at what God has done in the past:
  judging all his enemies.
9 He stops wars throughout the earth—
  shattering bows, breaking spears, burning shields.
10 He says, "Sit down and see who is in charge here:
  I am praised among the nations,
  praised throughout the whole earth."
11 The Lord of Armies is with us;
  the God of Jacob is our strong castle.

DAY 15

The God of Jacob Is Our Strong Castle

Think about your worst, most horrible day ever. I'm sure it was really bad and you were probably very sad, and maybe even hurt. But did the world end? No, the sun came up the next day, and you had to get up too.

But the writer of this psalm is thinking about a day when everything ends. The mountains become like jelly. The waves of the sea sweep over everything. That would be a really scary, really bad day, but this psalm tells us that even on that kind of bad day, God is looking out for us.

We all know this world is full of scary storms and scary people. Nations are growling at each other and wanting to fight. They are even getting their weapons ready. But this psalm doesn't focus on those things. It looks up, away from our scary world, and tells us to think instead about the heavenly city where God lives. In that beautiful, peaceful city, nothing bad ever happens.

When God raises his voice and shouts, "SIT DOWN!" everyone and everything has to obey him. Armies have to stop fighting. Diseases have to stop making us sick. People who stopped being our friends have to be our friends again.

The Lord of Armies is in charge of all things. But that doesn't mean he will always make our lives easy. We know this because he didn't give his own Son, Jesus Christ, an easy life either. When Jesus left the beautiful city in heaven and came down into this scary world of ours, he was very sad and hurt. God's enemies joined up to fight against Jesus, and God let them kill him.

But that was God's good plan. Because Jesus died on the cross and was raised back to life, he beat our very last enemy, death itself. People who trust in Jesus don't have to be scared to die. Death just means they leave this sad world to live with Jesus in the beautiful city where God rules forever.

Someday Jesus will make the earth as peaceful as his heavenly city. He will stop all wars and all sad things forever. We should say, "Come soon, Lord Jesus!" Until he does, let's ask him to be our strong and safe hiding place whenever we're in trouble.

Heavenly Father, sometimes living in this world really hurts us. It's sad and confusing and makes us cry a lot. Thank you, though, that this world isn't our true home. We belong in heaven with you, and we can't wait for the day when Jesus will come back and tell every bad thing to "SIT DOWN" once and for all. Until that happens, please be our safe and strong hiding place and help us keep our eyes fixed on you. Come, Lord Jesus! Amen.

PSALM 51:1-12

A psalm by David, after the prophet Nathan had
called him out for sinning against Bathsheba

[1] Please forgive me, God,

because of your faithful love;
because of your great kindness,

wipe out my failures.
[2] Thoroughly wash away my wrong actions

and clean away my sin,
[3] because I admit I did wrong,

and my sin is always in front of me.
[4] Against you alone I have sinned;

I did what is wrong before you;
you are absolutely correct to condemn me,

and you are right to judge me.

[5] I started off guilty already—

a sinner from before I was even born.
[6] You want honesty in the heart,

and you teach me wisdom deep inside me.

⁷ Splash me with clean water, and I will become clean;

wash me, and I will become whiter than snow.

⁸ Let me hear happy sounds;

let the bones you crushed dance for joy.

⁹ Look away from my sins,

and wipe all my guilt clean.

¹⁰ Give me a clean heart, God;

make my spirit new and eager to follow you.

¹¹ Don't kick me out of your presence;

don't take your Holy Spirit away from me.

¹² Give me back the joy that comes from being rescued

by you;

strengthen me so I want to obey you.

DAY 16

Please Forgive Me, God

Have you ever done anything so bad you didn't want to admit it? We all have. Even Christians can sin in big, bad ways, just like people who aren't Christians. But when Christians sin, we go to God and tell him we are truly sorry.

David wrote this psalm after he had hurt Bathsheba. Because he had broken God's rules, hurting Bathsheba was actually a sin against God! David was very sad and ashamed. He admitted what he had done wrong and asked God to forgive him. He asked God to make him clean instead of guilty, and he asked God to change him into a person who would eagerly *want* to follow God.

David knew he could go to God for help because God forgives really big sinners. He forgives us because of his faithful love. God treats Jesus's perfect goodness as if it were ours and treats the many sins we've committed against him as though Jesus had done them instead. It's like he has washed away all the dirtiness of our sin and made us cleaner than fresh snow.

God also gives us his Holy Spirit. Did you notice that? David asked God not to take his Spirit *away*, but he didn't have to be afraid. God *wants* us to have the Holy Spirit. The Spirit lives inside us to change our hard hearts and stubborn wills so we can obey God. We still have to fight against our sins all throughout our lives, but the day will finally come when those sins will all be completely gone.

That good news should make us very happy. We should sing, shout, and even dance for joy because of the great salvation Jesus has given us. And along with dancing and making the happy sounds, we should also go out and tell this good news to others—especially to those who have done bad things—so that they too can be forgiven, and made clean and new, by God.

Merciful Father, we are all awfully big sinners. We've all thought angry and mean thoughts and said things that we hoped would hurt other people. We have been jealous of things other people had and wanted those things to be ours instead. We all need your forgiveness, because our sin lies deep inside our hearts. Please forgive us for our many sins and help us look to Jesus and believe he's the one who rescues sinners. Wash us clean from our sin, and give us new hearts that want what you want—not what we want. Give us the joy we can have when we know that all our badness has been taken away and put on Jesus and that we are now your beloved children. We pray in his name, amen.

PSALM 62

A psalm by David

¹ I am waiting patiently for God,

　the one who rescues me.

² He is my rock and my salvation,

　my castle; I will not be tossed about—not much,

　anyway.

³ How long will you attack someone

　with murder in your minds,

　as if he were a leaning wall or a falling-down

　fence?

⁴ They make plans to knock me down from my high

　position.

　They love to trick people:

With their mouths they say kind things,

　but deep inside, they hate me.

⁵ I must wait patiently for God,

　on whom my hope rests.

⁶ He is my rock and my salvation,

　my castle; I will not be tossed about.

7 God saves me and honors me;

    my mighty rock, my castle, is God.

8 Trust him at all times, people;

    tell him all your hurts and needs,

    because God is our strong tower.

9 Human beings are just puffs of air;

    even important people are only a fairy tale:

When they are weighed, they all add up to nothing—

    they are only a breath.

10 Don't trust in bullying

    or put your hope in stealing;

    if you get more possessions, don't attach your heart

      to them.

11 God has said what he would do;

    we can count on these things:

You are powerful

    12 and faithful in your love, God, my Master.

You will certainly pay back everyone

    for what they have done.

DAY 17

I Am Waiting Patiently for God

Don't you love how honest David is in this psalm? He is being attacked from all directions by enemies who are trying to knock him down, and he says, "I will not be tossed about—not much, anyway"! He doesn't pretend that this attack isn't happening or that he doesn't notice it. He says that he feels shaken, the same way we would. But he doesn't feel *scared*.

David has planted his hope in God. That's why he doesn't feel scared. God is his salvation and his castle. God gives him a place to hide away from mean people. They're only human beings, and he knows they can't really hurt him. He says they're nothing more than a puff of wind. If you put them on a scale, what would they weigh? Nothing!

David trusts God so much because he knows two important things about him. First, God is powerful. Second, the people who serve him can count on his love for them. If we want to trust him the same way David did, we also need to trust that those two things are true.

God is powerful enough to rescue us, whenever he wants. He made everything, and he is in charge of everything too.

He's even in charge of our enemies. So we don't need to be scared of them: They can't touch us without his permission. And God will never leave us or forget about us, so we are safe in him. Even when scary or sad things happen, we can know for sure that God can use all the things that hurt us so that they end up being good for us.

Jesus proves that these things about God are true. Can you think of some powerful things he did? He stopped a storm, forgave people's sins, and even brought dead people back to life.* He also showed us that we can count on his love. After all, he could have escaped from the cross, but he allowed himself to die. Why? Because he loved us, and he knew that dying was the only way to save us.

When we believe in Jesus, God becomes our rock and our salvation. He rescues us and saves us, just as he saved David. We can trust in him and count on him, no matter what happens to us. He has the power to fix any problem, and because he loves us, he will make everything work out to be good for us in the end. We can trust in him at all times and cry out to him, because he hears our prayers.

> Mighty God, you are the one who saves us. Help us to trust in you when times are hard. Even when we are being tossed about like beach balls in the ocean, help us to keep trusting you. Thank you that we can count on you to love us and hold us tight, even when we are scared and weak. Thank you for sending Jesus to show us that this is true. Teach us to trust in you always, no matter what. Amen.

* Read Mark 4:39; Mark 2:5; and John 11:43 for examples.

PSALM 72:1-8

A psalm by Solomon

[1] God, please give wisdom to the king
    and goodness to the king's son.
[2] May he judge your people the right way
    and bring justice to those who are being bullied.
[3] May the farms grow lots of food for the people,
    and may the people do what is right.

[4] May the king give justice to those who are being hurt;
    may he rescue the children of the poor,
    but may he destroy those who hurt others.
[5] May your people respect you as long as the sun
    and moon still shine, throughout all time.

[6] May the king be like the rain falling on newly cut
    grass,
    like the springtime rain that gives the land the
    water it needs.
[7] May those who do what is right live happily and well
    as long as he is ruling,
    and may there be plenty for everyone, all the way
    until the moon is no more.
[8] May his kingdom stretch from ocean to ocean,
    from the Euphrates River to the ends of the earth.

DAY 18

Please Give Wisdom to the King

God promised to be with David's children and grandchildren, just as he had been with David.* When David's son Solomon became king after David, he wrote this psalm, Psalm 72, to ask God to make him wise and good. He wanted to judge all his people fairly, whether they were rich or poor, and rescue anyone who was being hurt. He also asked God to provide plenty of good things for everyone to enjoy. Most of all, he asked that he and the people of Israel would respect the Lord and follow in his ways. Wouldn't it be great to live in a country with such a wise and good king?

Solomon was a wise king, but he also made many mistakes. He didn't do everything that he hoped he would when he wrote this psalm . . . and most of the kings who came after him were worse than he was. Instead of stretching all the way to the ends of the earth, his kingdom was broken in half when his son became the next king.† And his son was a bad king who *really* wasn't what this psalm was praying for.

* See the promises God made to David in 2 Samuel 7.
† Read the whole crazy story in 1 Kings 12.

Does that mean God didn't answer Solomon's prayer? Actually, one day, he did! Which King do you think *was* the very good king this psalm asks for? Yes, it was Jesus! He is the true King who is perfectly wise and good. He judges all the people on the earth fairly. He especially cares about poor people and those who are being hurt, and he will rule forever: "as long as the sun and moon still shine"!

We can follow in God's ways and enjoy the good things our King gives us if we trust in Jesus. We need to tell our sins to him and ask him to forgive us. We need to ask him to help us do what is right. When we do this, we don't just become the people of his kingdom. We actually become his *children,* and we share the reward that God is giving to Jesus. We can look forward to the wonderful day when everyone will see how big and amazing Jesus's kingdom really is: the day he returns in glory to rule the whole world as its king.

Almighty God, thank you for King Jesus. Thank you that he is already ruling, even now, over all the nations. Thank you that he will not count up the many wrong things we have said and done against you but instead judge us based on whether we trust in him. Thank you that, because of Jesus, we'll live in heaven, where you will be pleased with us forever. Until we get there, please help the people who are in charge of us on earth to judge our nation wisely and fairly. Make our country peaceful so that we stay safe as we serve and respect you while waiting for King Jesus to come back. Amen.

* John 1:12.

PSALM 73:1-3, 12-28

A psalm by Asaph

¹ Isn't God good to Israel—
    to those who have good hearts?
² But my feet were slipping,
    and I almost tumbled off the path.
³ I became jealous of those who are boastful
    when I saw how well the bad people were doing.

¹² Look at those bad people:
    always comfortable and getting richer!
¹³ It seemed useless for me to keep my heart clean
    and wash my hands all the time.
¹⁴ All day long I have been hurting,
    and I am punished every morning.
¹⁵ If I had said things like this out loud,
    I would have let younger people down who look
        up to me,
¹⁶ but when I tried to figure out why bad people have
        it so easy,
    it seemed too hard to understand.
¹⁷ Until I went into God's temple, that is—
    then I understood where all this is heading.

[18] You have placed the bad people on a slippery path;
   you throw them down to destruction.
[19] They will soon be destroyed,
   completely swept away by terrifying things.
[20] Like someone waking up out of a dream, Master,
   you wake up and put them out of your mind.

[21] When my heart became angry
   and my feelings were hurt,
[22] I was stupid and wasn't thinking.
   I behaved like a silly animal before you.
[23] But even so, you are always with me,
   and you hold tight to my right hand.
[24] You guide me with your wise words,
   and you will take me to a glorious place when I die.
[25] Who else do I have in heaven?
   If I have you, I don't need anything else on earth.
[26] Of course, my body and spirit will come to an end,
   but God is the rock who protects me, and he is my
      reward forever.
[27] Those who are far from you will die;
   you destroy everyone who is unfaithful to you.
[28] For me, though, being near God is the best;
   I have made my Master, the Lord, my strong castle
   so that I can tell everyone all the things you have
      done.

My Feet Were Slipping

You might have noticed that this psalm says it's by "Asaph." That's because the book of Psalms is a songbook: It collects different songs that were written by different people. David wrote a lot of psalms, but this psalm was written by a man named Asaph.

Before he wrote this psalm, Asaph was angry. Did you notice why? It's because what he saw in the world around him didn't match what he thought the Bible was teaching him. Remember how Psalm 1 told us that good people will grow strong like green trees and bad people will all blow away? When Asaph looked around, he saw bad people getting rich and good people getting punished. Have you ever seen that?

Asaph was really upset. He felt sorry for the good people, and he felt angry at the bad people. But he also felt confused. If God said something would happen, but the opposite seemed to be happening, had God made a mistake? Was God *wrong* about good and bad people? And if he was, what *else* might God have been wrong about?

Asaph almost gave up on trusting God. But then he went into the temple and finally understood what was happening. He realized that what we *see* is not the whole story. Bad people may be having good lives now, but they are walking on a slippery pathway high up off the ground: At any moment, they may fall right off and die. Meanwhile, God is with his people, even when they are having a bad time: He holds our hands tightly and will not let us go. We can be *excited* when we think about the future. Being one of God's people who will live with him forever is much better than being rich.

What did Asaph see in the temple that changed his mind? He doesn't tell us. But I think it was probably the sacrifices. In the temple, priests killed and burned animals as offerings to God. Anyone who went to the temple to worship saw that something—or Someone—must die for us if we ever want to stand before God.

That wasn't all Asaph would have seen. The people in the temple also ate fellowship offerings. Those meals reminded them that God is making a forever feast for his people.

The sacrifices in the temple showed Asaph a better way to think. They show us something too. Like the animals that were killed in the temple, Jesus is the Lamb of God who was sacrificed for us. His death has taken away our sins so we can stand before God. The temple's fellowship offerings also remind us that a dinner is ready for us in heaven. In heaven, we will feast and celebrate that we can live with the Lamb forever. The things we have because of Jesus are much better than anything that bad people may get for a little while in this life—and what Jesus gives us will last forever!

Heavenly Father, help us see this world the right way. It is true that many bad people are happy and healthy while your people are sad and hurt. Help us not to be jealous of those who have more than we do. Instead, help us clearly see the wonderful reward that you have stored up for us in heaven. The good things that people can get in this world will not last, but the good things that you offer to us will. Help us trust that you will give us exactly what we need right now—whether we need a little or a lot. You are all we really need, and because of Jesus you are ours forever. Amen.

PSALM 78:1-8

A song by Asaph

1 My people, listen to my teaching;
    pay attention to my words.
2 I will speak wise sayings;
    I will explain old riddles,
3 things we learned from our grandparents.
4 We will not hide them from our children
    and grandchildren:
    We will tell the next generation
about God's amazing acts,
    his power and all the miracles he has done.
5 He wrote down the Ten Commandments for the
    people of Jacob
    and gave Israel laws
that he commanded our grandparents
    to teach their children.
6 So that the next generation—
    children who haven't even been born yet—
would be sure to tell their children,
    7 so that they would put their trust in God
and would not forget what he has done
    but would carefully obey his commands.
8 Then they will not be like their grandparents,
    who were stubborn and disobedient:
Their hearts were not committed
    and their spirits were not faithful to God.

DAY 20

We Will Tell the Next Generation About God's Amazing Acts

Families are very important to God's plan for the world. Most people trust in Jesus because their parents take the time to sit down with them when they are children and talk to them about God. Children are not supposed to have to figure things out about God on their own! That would make the gospel seem like a riddle that is hard to work out.

God tells us to teach our children and our grandchildren to know him. We can do this by helping them learn a couple of different lessons. To begin with, we should teach them the *history* of God and his people. This is the stories of all the amazing things that God did for Israel and has kept doing for his people ever since then. The second thing we should teach them is all the wise *laws* that God gave us. These laws are important to follow! But they also show us that we cannot follow them very well. When we see how bad we are, we see that we need Jesus to save us.

It may seem funny for you to think about having children and grandchildren someday. But you don't need to wait all the way until then to practice teaching others about God. You can start telling people about God's amazing acts and his wise laws right now. And you can listen to your parents, and to other people at church, when they tell you about these things. The more you listen and learn, the more you will be able to help others learn about God as well.

We don't want to be like people who forget God and are stubborn and disobedient. The psalm tells us about these kinds of people. They acted in ways that caused God to judge them. Instead of forgetting God, those people should have put their trust in God. After all, he is the one who can save us. In fact, he is the *only* one who can! And he saves us, and helps us to be true and loyal to him, when we trust in him.

Mighty God, your Old Testament people—people like Abraham, Isaac, and Jacob, Hannah, Ruth, and Esther—could always count on you to save them. Thank you that your New Testament people, the church, can count on you to save us too. We pray for anyone in our family who doesn't know you. Help us tell them the good news about Jesus and about our great God. Help us also tell these things to our friends, so that everyone in the whole world may know what a glorious and amazing God you are. Amen.

PSALM 84

A psalm by the sons of Korah

¹ I really love your house,
  Lord of Armies:
² I wish I could always be
  in the palace of the Lord!

My whole self cries out
  to the living God.
³ Even birds find homes in his house,
  and swallows make nests by your altars,
  where they can hatch their chicks,
Lord of Armies,
  my King and my God.

⁴ I wish I could live in your house
  and always praise you.
⁵ I admire all those who find their strength in you:
  those who are desperate to visit Jerusalem.
⁶ As they pass through the Valley of Tears,
  it becomes a place with plenty of water;
  The rain during the spring pours out good things
    on it.
⁷ These travelers build their strength back up
  until they can all appear before God at the temple.

[8] Lord God of Armies, hear my prayer;
    open your ears to me, God of Jacob.
[9] Look on our king with a smile, God;
    gaze at the face of your Chosen One.
[10] One day in your palace is better
    than a thousand days anywhere else;
I would rather stand at the doorway of the house of
    my God
    than live comfortably in the tents of bad people.

[11] For the Lord God is both a sun and a shield:
    He gives love and honor;
he doesn't keep anything good away
    from those who live honestly.
[12] I admire the person who trusts in you,
    Lord of Armies.

I Wish I Could Live in Your House

Have you ever gone on a vacation to visit a very special place? Trips like that can be fun—so much fun that we want to stay on vacation forever! Can you think of somewhere you would like to stay forever?

Every year, Israelites went on a trip to Jerusalem to worship God. It was a long, hard, dangerous journey. The Israelites even traveled through a place they called the Valley of Tears. But the writers of this psalm knew God could protect his people and make them strong as they walked to his temple. God could even take their tears and turn them into pools of water, helping many plants to grow.

After the people had worshiped at God's temple, they had to travel all the way back home. But the writers of this psalm wished they could stay in God's house forever, like the little birds that nested in the ceiling of the temple. They knew that being with God in his temple, even just for one day, was better than living for many years anywhere else. In fact, being at the very *edge* of God's house would be much better than living comfortably with people who reject God and love bad things.

Did you notice the other special prayer in this psalm? The writers wanted God's smile to shine down on the Messiah: the king God had chosen for Israel. If God smiled on this king, then the king would rule and lead his people well. Everyone would be happy.

We are also God's people, and we are following the perfect King he has chosen for us. But we don't have to make a long journey to Jerusalem to meet with God now. In fact, we don't have to go *anywhere* to try to get closer to him, because Jesus has brought God close to *us*. When we trust in him, Jesus makes us into God's temple. He lives inside us by his Spirit, which means God is with us all the time. God is even smiling on us, because he's smiling on that King he has chosen for us: King Jesus.

Even though we don't have to travel to the temple in Jerusalem to meet with God, our lives can sometimes feel like a Valley of Tears. But when we cry, none of our tears will be wasted. God will use all our sadness in ways that show us how great he is. Whatever happens will be good for us in the end.

When we die, God will bring us into his house where we can stay forever. There, in heaven, we'll be able to look into *God's* face with our own eyes, and we will shout with joy.

Heavenly Father, we are sorry that we don't always feel excited to see you the way the people of Israel did. When we go to church, we sometimes forget that you are there. When we meet other people who believe in you, we don't always see that they are temples that you are living inside, through your Holy Spirit. We don't think about how they are precious people you love and have saved. When we go through our own Valleys of Tears, please walk beside us and make us stronger. Be the sun that lights our way through life and the shield that protects us from all dangers. In Jesus's name, amen.

PSALM 88:1-5, 13-18

A psalm by the sons of Korah

1 Lord, God of my salvation,
   during the day I cry out to you, and at night I come
      before you.
2 Let my prayer come before you;
   listen to my cry.
3 I am full of troubles,
   and I feel like my life is over.

4 People think I am already too far gone,
   without help or hope;
5 I feel like I've been left among the dead—
   like the dead soldiers who sleep in the grave,
like those you don't remember anymore,
   who are cut off from your care.
13 But I still cry to you for help, Lord;
   in the early morning, my prayer goes up to you.

¹⁴ Why do you ignore me, Lord?

    Why do you hide your face from me?

¹⁵ I've had troubles and been close to death since

    I was a child.

    I suffer under your attacks, and there's nothing

    I can do.

¹⁶ Your anger sweeps over me;

    your terrors are killing me.

¹⁷ They surround me like deep water all day long;

    they close in on all sides.

¹⁸ You have kept my friends and neighbors away far

    from me;

    my whole life is a dark place.

DAY 22

I Feel Like My Life Is Over

Have you ever felt sad and lonely, like you didn't have a friend in the world? If you have felt that way, did it make you wonder if God still cared about you? Our psalm for today is the saddest of all the psalms because the writer feels like God has left him completely on his own. Other psalms, even the sad ones, end with a happy thought. But this psalm doesn't. Why do you think God gave us this psalm?

Sometimes we are very unhappy and can't cheer ourselves up. We pray and ask God to rescue us, but we are still sad. This good and important psalm gives us words we can use to talk about these hard times.

But God gave us this psalm for another important reason. He did it to prove that he had not forgotten the writer, even though the writer thought he had. Even though the writer was so sad and felt so alone, he still prayed to God—and God made sure to put this writer's psalm in our Bibles so we could remember him too.

God also knows exactly what it is like to be sad and alone. When Jesus went to the cross, all his followers left him: He was all by himself when God punished him for our sins. Jesus suffered under God's *attacks*–just like the writer of this psalm talks about. Jesus has prayed this psalm for us.

If we trust in Jesus, then even if we feel like our lives are over–in fact, even after we *have* died–death won't be the end for us. We know that because death wasn't the end for Jesus either. After Jesus suffered God's anger on the cross, God raised Jesus from the dead and took him up to heaven in glory. God ended Jesus's suffering when the time was right, and, if we belong to Jesus, he will end our own sad and hard times one day. On that day, we will join Jesus in his glory.

God will never leave us on our own. He will always care about us. The dark places will never be our final home, if we know the God who is light himself!

Lord, sometimes you feel very far away when we are sad and lonely. Help us keep calling out to you, even when we think you aren't listening. We pray for you to give us good friends who can encourage us when we are sad. And if we ever feel that we are alone and *don't* have even one friend in the world, please be close to us and remind us that you always love us for Jesus's sake. Thank you that Jesus went through the deepest darkness for us and that, because of him, the light of your face always shines on us–even during the darkest times that we go through. Amen.

PSALM 90:1-12

A psalm by Moses

[1] Master, you have been our safe hiding place
throughout all time.
[2] Before the mountains were made
or you shaped the earth and the world,
from that beginning all the way to the end, you
are God.

[3] You send weak human beings back to the dust,
saying, "Return, children of Adam."
[4] A thousand years
are like a single day for you—
they are not even as long as a night.
[5] You sweep people away, and they sleep in death;
in the morning, new grass springs up in their place.
[6] In the morning, that grass flowers and grows;
by the afternoon, it is shriveled up and dry.

[7] We are torn apart by your anger
    and frightened by your rage.
[8] You have laid out our sins in front of you
    and brought our secrets to light before you.
[9] All our days pass by under your judgment;
    we come to the end of our lives with a whisper.
[10] We may live to be seventy years old,
    or maybe eighty if we are strong,
but even our best moments are made up of trouble
    and sorrow.
        They pass away quickly, and then we fly away too.

[11] Who understands how powerful your anger is?
    Your fury makes people respect you.
[12] Teach us to count our days
    so that our hearts may be wise.

DAY 23

Who Understands How Powerful Your Anger Is?

Psalm 90 is the one psalm that we know Moses wrote. In it, he thinks about how short life is for human beings. It is short because God is angry with us and sends us back to the dust. But Moses also says that God is "our safe hiding place"! How is that possible?

First, let's think about why God is angry with us. *Sin* makes God angry. We sin a lot, so God is right to be angry with every single one of us.

Of course, we don't realize that the bad things we think and say and do are so very bad. Sin is a liar. It tells us that disobeying God will give us a better life. It tells us that we will have fun and be happy if we break God's rules. It tells us that God doesn't care what we do.

But sin doesn't bring us a better life. It doesn't make us happy. Instead, it pulls us away from God, the only one who can give us real life. If we don't learn this lesson by watching other people suffer for their sin, we will have to learn it by suffering ourselves.

Now let's think about why God is our safe hiding place. God knows that when he is angry with us, our sin makes us fight against him even harder. God knows that being kind and patient will make us sorry for our sin.*

God can be kind and patient with us because of Jesus Christ. Because Jesus died on the cross, his life on earth was much shorter than the seventy or eighty years Moses says are normal. Jesus understood exactly how powerful God's anger is because God punished him in our place. By dying for us, he made it possible for us to have life forever, just like God. Jesus was swept away and didn't see the Father's smile, so that the Father can give us his grace and smile on us instead.† That's the same grace that Moses counted on—and we can count on it too.

Jesus wasn't sent to the dust for ever. God raised him from the dead, like the grass that springs up. Now he is living with the Father in a special place forever. We can be sure that anything we do for him will not be wasted.‡ Even when we suffer on earth, we can be happy. Our days on earth will add up to only a small number, but we won't even be able to count the days we will spend in heaven with God.

Heavenly Father, even though this world is often a sad and hard place to live in, most people are still sorry to leave it when they die. Help us to face the truth about how many days we have, so that we can be wise. Remind

---

* Romans 2:4.

† Numbers 6:23–27 talks about how wonderful it is to have God's smile shine on us.

‡ 1 Corinthians 15:58.

us that our very best life won't come in this world but in heaven with you. We praise you that because of Jesus, you do not punish us the way that our sins deserve. Instead, you count us as good people and shine your goodness on us. Please make us more and more ready to live with you forever, no matter how many days we have to live on earth. Amen.

PSALM 95

[1] Come, let's give a noisy yell in praise of the Lord;

let's shout out loud to the Rock who saves us!

[2] Let's come before him with thankful hearts;

let's shout to him with songs of praise.

[3] For the Lord is a great God

and a great king over all gods.

[4] His hands hold the deepest parts of the earth,

and the very tops of the mountains are also his.

[5] The sea is his because he made it,

and his hands shaped the dry ground.

[6] Come, let's bow down to the ground in front of him;

let's kneel down before the Lord, our Maker.

[7] For he is our God,

and we are the people that he shepherds,

the sheep in his care.

If you people would only listen today to his voice!
    ⁸ Don't harden your hearts like you did at Meribah—
    like that day in the wilderness at Massah,
⁹ when your fathers tested me;
    they tried my patience, even though they had seen
    what I could do.
¹⁰ For forty years, I couldn't stand that generation;
    I said, "These people always wander off in their
    hearts;
    they don't know my ways."
¹¹ I was so angry about them that I made a promise:
    "They will never, ever enter my rest!"

DAY 24

Let's Come Before Him with Thankful Hearts

Have you ever gotten lost because you wandered away from your mom or dad? Maybe you went to look at something, then turned around later and realized you had no idea where your parents were. That is scary!

This psalm tells us that it's even scarier to wander away from God! The first part calls us all to come *to* the Lord, the God who made all things. It tells us to worship him by bowing down to him—and also by singing and even shouting to him! But the second part warns us not to wander *away* from him. That is what the people of Israel did long ago. God helped the Israelites escape out of Egypt. The Israelites saw God make a path through the Red Sea so they could be safe. But they started grumbling about him as soon as they came to desert places called Meribah and Massah and couldn't find any water to drink.*

What does this teach us? It teaches us that we will obey God the right way only if we're also worshiping him the right way. The Israelites hardened their hearts and

* Read this surprising story in Exodus 17.

complained about God because they stopped believing that he was the Shepherd who would protect them and give them what they needed. Because they wandered away from the Lord in their hearts, they wandered away from him in what they said and did. But sheep that wander away from their shepherd are always headed for disaster. They can't rest or be safe without their shepherd. That is why God himself says that those Israelites couldn't enter his rest.

How do we make sure our hearts are open to God and our ears are paying attention to his voice? We must remind ourselves, again and again, of what God has done for us. He beat the Egyptians' gods to set the Israelites free, and he led his people safely through the Red Sea. He sent Jesus Christ to be the Good Shepherd who died to protect his sheep. Jesus is alive again and standing next to the Father. He is praying for us, and he is the only one who can bring us to a good place where we can truly rest.

So let's shout praises to the Lord! Let's worship by singing to him loudly! Let's bow down to him and celebrate how much greater he is than any other god. He's the one who's really our Shepherd *and* our King!

Good Shepherd, thank you for the way you always take care of us. Forgive us for acting like sheep that wander away from you. Forgive us for bleating in our hearts that you aren't a good shepherd. Teach us to trust that, because you are our Shepherd, you are much wiser than we are. Teach us to believe that you will bring us to a place where we can finally rest and be safe. Help our hearts and voices to be delighted whenever we praise you. Amen.

PSALM 98

A psalm

1 Sing a new song to the Lord,
    because he has done miraculous things;
his strong right arm and his holy power
    have won him the battle.
2 The Lord has shown everyone his great power;
    he has revealed his justice in the sight of the nations.
3 He has acted on his faithful love
    to Israel;
The farthest corners of the earth have seen
    our God's victory.

4 Shout joyfully to the Lord, everyone on earth;
    burst out in noisy cries and sing!
5 Sing to the Lord with a harp;
    with a harp and the sound of singing;
6 with trumpets and by playing the ram's horn,
    shout loudly before the King, the Lord.

7 Let the sea and all who swim in it,
    as well as the earth and its creatures, roar for joy.
8 Let the rivers clap their hands
    and the mountains join together in loud singing
9 before the Lord, because he is coming
    to judge the earth:
He will judge the world justly
    and the peoples fairly.

Sing a New Song to the Lord

When the Bible talks about a *new song*, it's not talking about a song that someone just made up. It means a song celebrating something new that God has done for his people. When God saves his people in a new way, we write new songs about it.

That's why this psalm was written. God had just shown his power by rescuing his people from their enemies. The writer of the psalm responds by asking the whole world to celebrate what the Lord has done. And he doesn't just want *people* to praise God! He tells even the mighty seas and rivers to join this new song that he's singing.

At the end of the New Testament, in the book of Revelation, God's people in heaven sing another new song about a new way God has saved them. That beautiful new song celebrates Jesus, the Lamb of God who was killed so that we can live.* His blood washed away all our sins, and he has made people from all the nations—the farthest corners of the earth—into one family: the children of God.

* Revelation 5:9.

Our psalm for today also says that Jesus will come back someday to make everything that's wrong right and everything that's unfair fair again. On that day, he will wipe away every sad tear, and we will have a huge party. We will play music and sing to praise the Lord for beating sin and evil and death! The heart of every person who belongs to him will jump for joy when the Lord comes back. He is our King, and he has won the fight to save us.

Mighty King, you deserve to have great songs of praise sung about you because of your faithful love for your people. You helped your Old Testament people win in amazing ways, and you gave your New Testament people even more things to thank you for and songs to sing. Most of all, we should sing about how you've saved us through Jesus. Give us joyful and thankful hearts that want to sing your praises, and help us spread the good news about Jesus to the farthest corners of the earth. We pray in Jesus's name, amen.

PSALM 100

A psalm for saying "Thank you"

¹ Let the whole world shout triumphantly to the Lord!

² Serve the Lord joyfully;

come before him with yells of delight!

³ Remember that the Lord is the only God;

he made us, and we belong to him;

we are his people and the sheep that he cares for.

⁴ Go in through his palace gates with thanksgiving,

and enter his courtyards with praise;

thank him and glorify his name.

⁵ For the Lord is good,

and his faithful love lasts forever;

his faithfulness continues to all generations.

DAY 26

Serve the Lord Joyfully

An old songbook took the part of this psalm that says, "Serve the Lord joyfully," and changed it to say, "Serve him with fear" instead. That's a big difference! It's almost as if someone thought this psalm was *too* happy. It's as if someone wanted everyone to calm down and be serious instead of happy.

But being joyful is the whole point of Psalm 100: It shows us a crowd that's going crazy with happiness. The person who first wrote this psalm wanted the whole world to praise God by singing to him with joyful hearts. Praising God should be a happy celebration. David gives us a good example. He danced with joy when he brought God's special ark of the covenant home to Jerusalem.*

The psalm tells us a very simple reason we should have all this joy. The Lord is the only God. The gods that other people worship are only pretend—they aren't real. The psalm also tells us that the Lord made us and chose us to belong to him in a special way. He is our King, and we are his

* You can read this story in 2 Samuel 6.

people. He is the Good Shepherd, and we are the sheep that he always looks after. Our God rules over everything–and his rule is always good for his people! He invites us to sing and celebrate because he rules over us. We can thank him for the love and kindness he's always showing to us and to our children and grandchildren as well.

If God's people long ago could get so excited about how he loved and cared for them, how much more excited should we be? Now that Jesus has come, God's people aren't just the people from Israel anymore. Now men and women and boys and girls from all over the world belong to God.

When we come before God by going to church, we don't need to act sad as though we're at a funeral. Yes, someone *did* die–when love took Jesus to the awful cross so that he could die for our sins. But Jesus didn't stay dead! He is alive again, and he is King over everything. So sing, shout, dance, and celebrate your King! Tell your children and grandchildren the exciting story one day! And don't let anyone tell you to be quiet when you are praising and celebrating him.

Mighty God, you rule over all things in a way that's always good for your people. You even rule over death, which means nothing can keep us away from your love. Help us delight in this good news and shout your praises with great joy. Make us really want to see other people come to know you, our God, the way we do. May the whole earth shout about how you have won and bring you all the glory you deserve. In Jesus's name, amen.

PSALM 103:1-14

By David

¹ Let me be the first to praise the Lord;

everything that I am,

praise his holy name!

² Let me be the first to praise the Lord;

I don't want to forget anything he has done for me!

³ He forgives all my sins

and heals all my diseases.

⁴ He buys my life back from Death;

he crowns me with faithful love and mercy.

⁵ He gives me so many good things

and makes me feel young again—so young I could

soar like an eagle.

⁶ The Lord does what is right

and gives justice to all those who are being hurt.

⁷ He showed himself to Moses,

and the Israelites saw what he could do.

[8] The Lord shows mercy and is kind;
    he is slow to get angry and full of love we can rely
        on;
[9] he will not always criticize us
    or stay angry forever.
[10] He has not treated us the way our sins deserve,
    nor has he paid us back for the wrong things we
        have done.

[11] As high as the heavens are above the earth,
    so big is his faithful love to those who fear him.
[12] As far as the east is from the west,
    that's how far he's taken our sin away from us.
[13] The way a father shows kindness to his children
    is how the Lord shows kindness to those who fear
        him;
[14] he knows what we are made of
    and remembers that we are only dust.

DAY 27

He Forgives All My Sins

If you made a list of all the good things God has done for you, what would you put on it?

When David wrote this psalm, he thought of many reasons for us to love and thank our God. The psalm reminds us that God rescues us from danger and heals us when we are sick. He gives us good gifts and always does what is right. He knows how weak we are, and so he is gentle with us—just like someone who is very careful not to drop a baby. Can you think of some ways that God has rescued or healed you? Can you think of some ways that he treats you gently?

David also mentions a *really* big reason that he loves and praises God. Did you notice what it is? He wants to celebrate the mercy and forgiveness that God shows us. We have sinned against God and tried to fight with him, over and over again. We have thought, said, and done many things that he tells us not to, but he forgives us and shows us his grace over and over again too.

At the end of the day, does the sun go down in the same place where it came up in the morning? No! It goes all the way to the other side of the sky—and that long distance is how far God takes our sins away from us. You can't get any farther than that! He has shown us mercy and forgiven us since way back when time began, and he'll keep doing it all the way until the end. We can rely on his love to last forever. What has God forgiven you for? What has he done to show you his amazing love?

This is why we should praise the Lord with our whole hearts. Every day we can think of more good things he has done for us, and we can love him more and more for his kindness to us and to the whole world. Yes, we are very weak, but he is good and kind and wise. He is a merciful Father and a perfect King. He is a forgiving and loving God. Praise his holy name!

Glorious Father, we praise and love you very much today because of who you are and what you have done for us. We are very weak and foolish, and we often don't obey you or respect you. But you always show us mercy and kindness. You forgive our many sins for the sake of Jesus. We pray that you would make us into the people we ought to be. Please never stop forgiving us because we'll always need new mercy from you every single day. Help us love and praise you the way we should and sing your praises all the time. You are the most amazing God! Amen.

PSALM 111

^{1} Praise the Lord!
I will give thanks to the Lord with all my heart,
   whenever I get together to worship him with his
   people.
^{2} The Lord's actions are amazing,
   and those who love him think about them often.
^{3} He does incredible things,
   and his goodness lasts forever.
^{4} His miraculous acts are unforgettable;
   the Lord shows mercy and is kind.
^{5} He provides food for those who fear him;
   he remembers his promises forever.
^{6} He showed his people what his power can do:
   He gave them a land that had belonged to other
   nations.
^{7} His actions are faithful and just;
   all his rules are dependable.
^{8} They will keep being true forever and ever,
   and we should keep them faithfully and honestly.
^{9} He has saved his people;
   he makes sure that his promises will be kept
   forever—
   his character is holy and awesome.

^{10} Showing respect to the Lord is where wisdom begins;
   those who obey him are smart.
   His praise will last forever.

DAY 28

The Lord's Actions Are Amazing

A long time ago, the Lord made a promise to the people of Israel. He said that he would be their God and that they would be his people.

The Old Testament is filled with stories that show how much the Israelites could count on God to keep his promise. He brought them out of the land of Egypt. He pushed the Red Sea apart in front of them so that they could cross to the other side safely. He brought them to live in a land that had lots of food for them to eat. He helped them win against the bad people who lived in the land. When the people sinned so much that they lost the land and became slaves in faraway Babylon, God brought them back home once again, just as he had said he would.

The Lord always keeps his promises—and many times he keeps them by doing amazing things! The psalm says those amazing things show his people what his power can do. They also show his people why they should trust him and do what he calls us to do.

But God made another promise. This promise might be his biggest and most amazing promise of all. Even before

God chose the Israelites and made them his people, he told Adam and Eve that he would send someone to beat our enemies. He chose Jesus Christ to fight for us, and Jesus won the fight when he died on the cross and came back to life three days later. That's the *most* amazing and incredible thing the Lord has done. It's the miracle he did to save his people forever.

What else can you thank the Lord for doing? Praise him for the holy and awesome things he has done!

Almighty God, we thank you for the wonderful things the Bible shows us you have done for our sake. You saved your people from their enemies and gave them a land to live in. When they sinned against you, you forgave their sins. Now we are also your people, forever, because you kept your promise and sent your own Son to die in our place. Thank you for all the kindness and mercy you have shown to your people in the Bible—and to us. Help us trust your promises, respect your wisdom, and obey your Word. In Jesus's name, amen.

PSALM 115

[1] Not to us, Lord, not to us but to your name be
   the glory,
   because of the love that we know you always
   show us.
[2] Why should the nations ask,
   "Where is their God?"
[3] Our God is in heaven,
   and he does whatever he wants.

[4] Their idols are just silver and gold;
   they've been made by people's hands.
[5] Those idols have mouths but can't speak;
   eyes, but they can't see;
[6] they have ears but can't hear;
   noses, but they can't smell;
[7] they have hands that can't touch
   and feet that can't walk:
   They can't even make a sound.
[8] People who make idols are just like them;
   so is everyone who trusts in them.

⁹ Israel, trust in the Lord:

He is their helper and shield.

¹⁰ Aaron's children, trust in the Lord:

He is their helper and shield.

¹¹ You who fear the Lord, trust in the Lord:

He is their helper and shield.

¹² The Lord remembers us and will show us his favor:

He will show Israel his favor;

He will show Aaron's children his favor;

¹³ He will show his favor to those who fear the Lord,

from the youngest to the oldest.

¹⁴ May the Lord make your family larger

in each generation.

¹⁵ May the Lord, the Maker of heaven and earth,

show you his favor.

¹⁶ The heavens belong to the Lord,

but he has given the earth to the children of Adam.

¹⁷ It is not the dead who praise the Lord,

and it's not anyone who goes down to the silent

place.

¹⁸ As for us, we will praise the Lord,

from this moment on and forever.

DAY 29

To Your Name Be the Glory

When the Israelites were slaves in Babylon, the people of Babylon made fun of them. Why? Because the Israelites had an invisible God.

The Babylonian people thought their gold and silver idols were gods who helped them beat their enemies. They worshiped them and built beautiful temples for them. But had their idols really helped them? Not at all! Those idols hadn't done anything. They *couldn't.* They were just lumps of metal. The Lord is the one who controls everything.

God told his people not to listen to the silly bragging of their enemies. *He* was the one who had allowed the Babylonians to defeat them and take them away to be slaves. He had warned his people that this would happen if they didn't stop disobeying him, but they hadn't listened. But God had also promised that he would bring the people back to their homes again one day. He told them to trust him while they waited.

Like the people of Israel, we often don't listen to God either. Because he is invisible, we forget about him. We try to make other people happy instead of obeying God.

We worry about things that can't hurt us, and we trust in things that can't help us. We believe people when they say that *they* are in control.

Did you notice that this psalm reminds us again and again to trust God–and doesn't say we should trust anything else? But even all that reminding still isn't enough for us. We forget God anyway, but he still remembers us. In fact, our psalm today says that God even shows us his *favor*. That means that God will help us. That is very good news.

This psalm talks about Aaron's children. Who was Aaron? He was a priest, and so were his sons. Priests told Israel that the Lord was smiling on them and showing them his favor. God shows us his favor because of Jesus, and, just like Aaron and his children, Jesus blesses us. He is our Great High Priest. It is what *he* thinks about us that really matters, because he made the whole world and everything in it. He is in control of everything that happens. He is the one we should praise and worship.

Almighty God, you made everything out of nothing, and you decide everything that happens: big or small. Forgive us for acting as if other people and things are more important than you are. You are the only God. You deserve all our worship because you are always kind to us and we can always count on you—even when our lives are hard. Thank you for the many good gifts you give us. Amen.

PSALM 118:21-29

²¹ I will give you thanks because you answered

my prayer

by saving me.

²² The stone that the builders threw away

has become the most important stone of all.

²³ The Lord did this,

and we can see it was a miracle.

²⁴ The Lord brought about this special day;

that's why we are thrilled and full of joy.

²⁵ Oh Lord, save us!

Oh Lord, help us to win!

²⁶ May God show that he is on the side of the person

who comes in his name;

since we are in God's house, we will ask him to

show you his favor.

²⁷ The Lord is God,

and he shines his smile upon us;

tie the festival sacrifice

to the altar with ropes!

²⁸ You are my God, and I will give thanks to you;

you are my God, and I will lift you up!

²⁹ Give thanks to God: He is good,

and we can count on his love to last forever.

DAY 30

The Most Important Stone of All

Our God is always doing things that we don't expect. He takes the people who others don't want and makes them his own special people. The stone that builders don't want becomes the most important stone in his building. The Lord smiles with favor on his people—even when they don't deserve it. Why do you think God likes to do things that surprise us?

God did something else that surprised people, even though he had already told them he was going to do it: He promised that he would send us his Chosen One, but when that Chosen One came, *Jesus* surprised people the most—because they weren't expecting him at all. The Bible says that many people didn't think Jesus seemed like anyone special.* He was born in a little town, and no one knew much about him for many years. When he started to preach and teach, many people didn't listen to what he was saying. In fact, they even hated him and wanted to stop him from being their king.

* If this sounds hard to believe, Isaiah 53:1–3 tell us that it's true.

That is why Jesus said this psalm was actually talking about him. *He* was the stone that people wanted to throw away, but God would use him as the foundation stone to build his house.* We can rejoice because the Lord has answered our prayer and saved us. His favor shines on us, and he gives us his lovely smile!

The Lord gives us more and more to be surprised about. Why should he be kind to us when we are weak and don't obey him? We don't seem like the ones he would pick to be his people. But even though we often fail—and even if other people don't want us to be on their team—the Lord is still our God. The Bible says that he has forgiven our sins and made us into stones in his house.† He will love us forever because of Jesus—and this psalm says we can count on him completely!

Mighty Lord, you love to work through people who are weak and broken. Thank you that, through Jesus, you became weak and broken like us—but never sinned. Even though your own people didn't want you, Lord, you still love all those who belong to you and have saved us from our sins. Thank you for making us able to believe in you and to become part of your people, even though we don't deserve it. What an amazing thing you have done for us! Thank you that we can count on your love to watch over us forever. Amen.

---

* Jesus even quotes this psalm in Matthew 21:42.
† If you don't feel like a stone, just read 1 Peter 2:4–5!

PSALM 119:1-11

1 Happy are the people who always do what is right
   and obey God's law.
2 Happy are the people who keep the Ten
      Commandments
   and who seek God with all their hearts.
3 They don't do anything bad;
   instead they walk in God's ways.
4 You have told us that your instructions
   should be followed carefully—
5 if only the things I do would be perfectly
   in line with your instructions!
6 Then I wouldn't be ashamed,
   because I study your commands;
7 I would thank you, with a heart that means it,
   whenever I learn about your righteous rules.
8 I want to keep your instructions—
   please don't let go of me!
9 How can a young person keep walking on the path
      that makes sure they do only what's right?
   By guarding their way according to your Word.
10 I search for you with my whole heart—
   don't let me wander away from your commands!
11 I have kept your sayings in my heart, like a treasure,
   so I may not sin against you.

DAY 31

I Want to Keep Your Instructions

God made each one of us. Because he made us, he knows exactly how we should live. He wants *us* to know how we should live too, so he gave us his law with its rules and instructions that tell us what's right and wrong. Can you think of some of the rules in God's law?

Our verses for today come from Psalm 119. Psalm 119 is a really, really long poem! It needs to be very long to show how much the writer loves God's law. It tells us that God's law is wise, holy, and just. It says that we will be happy if we always do what's right and obey God's law.

There is a problem, though: Even if we want to work hard and keep God's instructions, we can't. Ever since Adam and Eve's first sin, no matter how hard we try, we can't obey God's law perfectly. We all know that if God judged us based on how well we obey his law, he would toss us in the garbage.

Even the writer of Psalm 119 realized he couldn't follow God's instructions perfectly. He failed at keeping them even though he treated them like priceless treasure. He wrote that he *wanted* to obey them, and he wished that he could, but he couldn't without help. He was ashamed about all the times that he wandered away and sinned against God. Sinning is a very big problem, because God tells us that we must keep his law perfectly if we don't want to die.

But God solved that problem for us. We can never obey perfectly, so God sent his own Son, Jesus, to keep God's commands and rules for us. Jesus obeyed God perfectly, and when we trust in him, God counts his goodness and obedience as ours. He takes away our failure to follow his rules, and he gives us Jesus's perfect obedience. Now God will never let go of us, and we don't have to die.

When we trust in Jesus, we *want* to keep God's instructions. We try hard to obey his law because we are *thankful* to God—not because we're afraid he'll let go of us or that he'll love us only if we do well. We try to obey his commands because they make us feel *joy* and we know they are good for us, not because we are afraid. Because of Jesus, we can be counted as happy people: people who always do what's right and obey God's law perfectly! What good news!

Holy Father, your law is perfect, wise, and good, but we can never keep it perfectly . . . and we often break it on purpose. Please forgive us for all the ways and times that we fail you and disobey. Help us look at Jesus, the one who kept your law perfectly for our sake. Teach us to trust that his perfect obedience is what will save us—not anything that we can do. And help us love your Word and your rules more and more, the way the writer of Psalm 119 did. In Jesus's name, amen.

PSALM 121

A song for the journey up to Jerusalem

¹ I look up at the hills;

who will help me when I am in danger?

² The Lord who made the heavens and the earth

will help me.

³ He won't let your foot slip;

he won't be caught napping.

⁴ The one who guards Israel

doesn't nap or sleep.

⁵ The Lord is your guard;

the Lord is right beside you and is shading you

from the hot sun.

⁶ The sun will not hurt you during the day,

and neither will the moon at night.

⁷ The Lord will guard you from all danger;

he will guard your life.

⁸ The Lord will guard you

when you go out and when you come home again,

both now and forever.

DAY 32

Who Will Help Me?

On day 21, we read about how the people of Israel made a dangerous journey to Jerusalem each year to celebrate and worship God. On their journey, they would sing this psalm, Psalm 121. As they looked up at the high hills they had to climb, they thought about how hard their journey would be. Who would take care of them on the way there?

The answer, of course, is the Lord. The psalm reminds us that he made the heavens and the earth. That means he also made the highest hills! God could protect the travelers as they climbed up and down and followed the long road all the way to the city of Jerusalem.

We are also on a journey. As we live our lives as God's people, we are walking on a path that will take us to the new Jerusalem in heaven. Though that journey is hard, God will hold us firmly in his strong hand. He sees every danger. He never sleeps when we need him. He never stops protecting us. He is right beside us. He is with us during the day and during the night. When we go outside and when we come back in—and every second in between—he watches over us. He will watch over us forever.

Life is often scary and dangerous, but we don't need to be scared! We can't always protect ourselves. Often we don't pay attention and wander into bad places. But the Lord takes care of us. He guides every step of our journey, until the day he welcomes us into his house forever. We don't have to be afraid of anything in heaven or on earth.

Keeping us safe cost God a lot. The Father had to *stop* protecting his own Son: He had to hand Jesus over to people who hated him and hurt him. They nailed him to the cross, and the Father let them do it. They mocked Jesus and made fun of his pain as the cross slowly took his life away. It seemed he had no one who would help him or take care of him.

But we all know this was not the end of the story, don't we! Jesus won the battle over death and rose back out of his grave. Now he's sitting beside the Father in heaven. Because he died so we wouldn't have to, Jesus help us and guards us from heaven. Because the Father didn't protect his Son, he now calls us his children and protects *us* forever. He will watch over us at all times, without ever taking a break, until he brings us safely home to heaven.

Jesus, thank you for choosing to take all the pain and hurt that we deserved to feel and putting it on yourself instead. Thank you for becoming our helper and our guard forever. Thank you that you never fall asleep or forget about us. Thank you that wherever we go and however long we live in this world, you will always be right beside us. When all we see is a dangerous path, help us look up to see you, our Savior and Lord, and know you are watching over us. Amen.

PSALM 122

A song for the journey up to Jerusalem; by David

[1] I was so excited when people said to me,

"Let's go up to the Lord's house."

[2] Our feet are actually standing

inside your gates, Jerusalem!

[3] Jerusalem is a united city,

where everyone lives together as a happy family.

[4] This is where the Lord's tribes go up,

as God commanded Israel,

to give thanks to the Lord's name.

[5] It's where the thrones of David's house are set up,

ready to give justice.

[6] Pray for Jerusalem to do well;

and may those who love you, Jerusalem, be safe.

[7] May things be at peace inside your walls

and good inside your fortresses.

[8] Because of my family and friends,

I will say, "Peace be within you."

[9] Because of the temple of the Lord our God,

I will seek your good.

DAY 33

Pray for Jerusalem to Do Well

Do you ever feel bored at church? Maybe you always see the same people. Maybe you always sing the same songs or read the same verses from the Bible. Can you imagine growing up a long time ago, back when this psalm was written? Back then, God's people went to special festivals each year in Jerusalem, also known as Zion. Imagine waiting your whole life to be old enough to go up to the city and join the festival yourself. How would you feel when you finally got to make the trip?

Imagine being in a huge crowd of people—more people than you've ever seen in your entire life. Imagine packing into the city together to praise the Lord. Imagine seeing the king's throne and the huge temple. Imagine watching as sacrifices are given to God. Imagine listening as people sing beautiful songs of worship. What a delight! You would be as excited as David was in our psalm today.

Jerusalem was an exciting place to visit every year. But it wasn't always a *safe* place. Sometimes enemy armies came to fight it. They wanted to destroy the city and its beautiful temple. God's people prayed that Jerusalem would be at peace. That way, they would stay safe as they traveled to it and worshiped God together.

Nowadays, we don't travel to a special city to meet with God. God comes to us. Whenever we meet with his people in church, he is with us through his Holy Spirit. Our churches may not feel as exciting as the temple in Jerusalem during a festival, but we have something that the writer of this psalm would have loved to see. Can you guess what it is?

By dying and rising back to life, Jesus has brought many people together to live as a happy family. Those *people* are his church. Those people are the Lord's house. Just like David prayed for Jerusalem, we can pray that God's church would to do well and be at peace.

It gets even better. Every Sunday when we go to worship, in an important way we are actually going to the Mount Zion in heaven and meeting with *God*.* Because Jesus's blood washed our sins away, God welcomes us to worship him in heaven—even when we're on earth. So whenever we go to church to worship, we can be just as excited as David!

God of all times and places, you lived with your people long ago in the temple in Jerusalem, and now you have come to live with us. Thank you that Jesus allows us to come before you as your forgiven children. Help us to love the church that we go to and to be excited to meet with you there, week after week. Remind us to pray that for your church to be at peace. Help us to love the other people in our church because they are part of a family together with us. In Jesus's name, amen.

* Hebrews 12:22–24 describes this.

PSALM 124

[1] If the Lord hadn't been on our side—

    let Israel say this—

[2] if the Lord hadn't been on our side

    when people attacked us,

[3] they would have swallowed us alive,

    they were so angry with us;

[4] the water would have flooded over us;

    the rushing river would have reached up to

      our necks;

[5] the raging waters would have

    drowned us!

[6] Praise the Lord,

    who didn't leave us

    to be chewed up by those angry people's teeth;

[7] we escaped like a bird

    from a hunter's net:

The net tore,

    and we got away.

[8] Our help is in the name of the Lord,

    who made the whole world.

DAY 34

If the Lord Hadn't Been on Our Side . . .

What do you think had just happened when David wrote this psalm? It sounds like some very powerful enemies had come after Israel, doesn't it? Those enemies wanted to swallow up God's people in one big angry bite. It looked like no one could save them. But then what do you think happened? Who came to help?

Yes, just when things were really scary, God stepped in. He rescued his people. He set them free as though they were birds that had been trapped in a net. This is why David tells Israel to sing, "Our help is in the name of the Lord."

Christians have also been rescued in an amazing way. We weren't just trapped. We were *dead* because of our sin. Our bad thoughts, words, and actions had swallowed us alive. We couldn't do anything to save ourselves.* But God stepped in. He didn't leave us to be chewed up by our sin. Instead, he took the punishment for all that sin and broke sin's power over us.†

* Ephesians 2 tells us about this bad situation.
† Romans 6:14.

But we need God's help more than once. We need his help every day! That's because, even though God rescued us from sin, we still sometimes climb right back into sin's net. Sometimes we *want* to go back and do something wrong. When we fall into sin all over again, the escape God has made for us is still there. The net can never trap us forever.*

David and the Israelites praised the Lord when he rescued them. We should praise him too, because he has saved us through Christ Jesus. If we are ever tempted to climb back into sin's net, Jesus can help us stay away from it. When we sin, we can run to God and tell him that we're sorry and want to stop. He will forgive us and give us a way out of sin. Praise the Lord! He is on our side and didn't leave us trapped in sin!

Mighty Lord, thank you for helping and rescuing us You made everything in this world. No one and nothing can harm us without your Fatherly permission. Thank you for not letting our sins swallow us alive. Thank you for forgiving us when we say and think and do bad things. Thank you for rescuing us from sin's trap—and for leaving us with a way out, when we sometimes try to climb back in. Thank you for the work you are doing in us and through us by your Holy Spirit. Amen.

* Paul tells us this in 1 Corinthians 10:13.

PSALM 127

A song for the journey up to Jerusalem; by Solomon

1 If the Lord isn't the one who builds a house,
the people who try to build it are wasting their
time.
If the Lord isn't watching over a city,
the ones who are guarding it shouldn't bother to
stay awake.
2 Getting up early,
staying up late,
and working really hard are all useless without him:
The Lord gives sleep to those he loves.

3 Children are a gift from the Lord;
having them is a reward from him.
4 Like a soldier's arrows
are sons born when someone is young:
5 Happy is the man
who has many of them;
he has backup
when he speaks to his enemies.

DAY 35

All Useless Without Him

Hard work is not enough. Cleverness is not enough. We need the Lord's favor if we want anything we try to go well. Do you remember what his favor means? It means he will help us.

When we are trying to build a house, get good grades, make money, keep something safe, or do anything else we want to do, we can get up early, stay up late, and work really, really hard. We can try to do those things the right way, but if God is not with us to help us do them, all our work will be useless. While we are staying up late and wasting our time, the people the Lord loves will be lying happily in their beds. They can sleep well because they trust him.

We also need the Lord's favor in order to have a family. The Lord decides when people have children. He decides if they will even have children at all. He decides whether those children will be boys or girls. This psalm talks about sons because, back when it was written, boys would help their dad if he was in an argument with another family in their town. But whether they are boys or girls, all children are a special reward from the Lord. We need God to give them to us as a gift. Parents can't just decide to have children and then make them appear!

The happiest family is a family in which Mom and Dad and all their children know and love the Lord. Parents can pray for this to happen. They can work hard and teach their children about Jesus. But in the end, only God can make sure the whole family loves him. *He* is the one who can give us the new hearts we need in order to love him. *He* is the only one who can save us.

Building a house can be good. Watching over a city can be good. But we should all want to be people who trust in the Lord—and we should want our children and grandchildren and everyone we know to trust him as well.

Dear Lord, we so often forget that all our work is useless without you. Forgive us for trusting that we can get things done on our own. Thank you that when we count on you to help us, we can rest instead of always trying harder and harder. We know that children are a gift from you too. We pray for people—especially in your church—who would love to have children but don't yet, and we ask you to give them this good gift. Please help parents to love their children well and to tell them about Jesus every day. We pray that parents would depend on you to give their children the new hearts they need to truly worship you. Amen.

PSALM 130

A song for the journey up to Jerusalem

[1] I cry to you for help because I am in deep waters, Lord:

[2] Lord, hear my cry!

Listen to me

when I call out for mercy!

[3] If you, Lord, kept a list of our sins,

who could face your judgment?

[4] But you are a God who forgives,

and you do it so that people may honor you.

[5] I wait for the Lord—my whole self waits for him;

I put my hope in his Word.

[6] My whole self waits for the Lord,

more than lookouts long for the dawn—

more than lookouts long for the dawn.

[7] Israel, hope in the Lord,

for the Lord is a God of faithful love

and amazing rescues.

[8] He himself will rescue Israel

from all their sins.

DAY 36

I Cry to You for Help, Lord

Have you ever felt really bad because you did something wrong? Maybe it made your stomach hurt. Maybe you couldn't sleep. Maybe you kept thinking about what you did and wishing you'd done something else. Maybe you felt scared about what might happen to you.

Our psalm today tells us that this bad, guilty feeling is like *drowning*. It feels like having deep water come right up over our heads. When we feel scared or sick or wide-awake because of something we've done wrong, we can cry out to the Lord for help. That's what this psalm's writer did. God will hear us when we tell him we're sorry. He will listen to us when we ask for his mercy.

Sometimes we want to keep a count of everything people do wrong. Have you ever watched someone to keep track of every new mistake they made so you could bring it up to them again? The psalm calls this keeping a *list* of sins. Sometimes other people do that to us. But the Lord is not like that. When we ask, he forgives us for every one of our sins. He forgives us whether we sinned long before or are sinning now. He will even forgive us for all the sins we haven't sinned yet. So if we start to think that we are too bad for God to love us, or that we can't go to him because we've done such awful things, this psalm tells us we are wrong. The Lord is the God of mercy. He wants us to come to him. He will never let us down when we trust in him.

God doesn't make a list of our sins. Is that because he forgets to write all our sins down? No! If that was all that happened, we would be scared that God would someday remember our sins and punish us! No, God's mercy means that he also *rescues* us from all our sins. Jesus paid the price for our sins that we should have paid. He paid that price completely. When he was done, he said, "It is finished."* So when your bad, guilty feelings won't leave you alone, you can say, "It is finished! God himself has rescued me from all my sins!" And you can be sure that it's true!

> Lord God, we sin against you many times each day. We can't even keep a list of all our sins, because we sin more times than we can count! Thank you that *you* don't count our sins either. Thank you that, through Jesus, you have paid the whole price for them. Thank you that you forgive us for every single one of them. Please help us hate our sin and turn away from it. And help us not to keep a list of other people's sins but to forgive them the same way we've been forgiven by you. You are truly an awesome God! Amen.

* He gives us this happy news in John 19:30.

PSALM 131

A song for the journey up to Jerusalem; by David

¹ My heart is not proud,
    and I don't look down on people;
I don't worry about things
    that are too hard to understand or ideas that are
      beyond me.
² I am calm and quiet
    like a toddler in his mother's arms;
    like a little child in his mother's arms, I am at peace.
³ Israel, put your hope in the Lord
    from now on and forever.

DAY 37

I Am Calm and Quiet

Grown-ups spend a lot of time thinking about what will happen tomorrow. They often worry and try to make plans for the future. But tiny children enjoy what's happening right now. That is a great gift! Little children get to run and play and have fun. They can enjoy what's happening right now. Mom and Dad are taking care of them today. They don't worry whether Mom and Dad will take care of them tomorrow too.

Psalm 131 says that, in this way, *all* of us can act like little children. We don't have to win at everything we do. We don't have to prove that we're better than other people. We don't have to know the answers to all our questions. We don't have to see what will happen in the future. Instead, we can rest in our heavenly Father's arms and be at peace. Like a toddler snuggled up to his mother, we can leave the hard things to God. We don't have to worry whether he will take care of us. We know that he will.

Of course, this works only if God is powerful and good. God loves us and cares about us. He is king over everything and wants what is best for us. Everything is under his loving control. That's why we don't need to worry about what's going to happen.

When Jesus lived on earth, he said that anyone who wanted could come into his kingdom. Anyone who wanted could be a part of his family and could live in heaven with him. But first, he said, they had to become like a little child.* He meant that the door of his kingdom is open to all the people who put their faith in him. He will accept all the people who trust him to care for them and be in charge of their lives. It doesn't matter if they are little and weak. Jesus is more than strong enough to take care of them.

But Jesus will not accept everyone. Some people are proud of themselves. They think they are better than other people. They want God to answer all their questions before they trust him. Those people are too puffed up to fit through the door of Jesus's kingdom.

Don't be like those people! Put your hope in God.

Heavenly Father, thank you that you love us. Thank you that we can snuggle down into your arms. Thank you that we can leave everything that's hard to you for you to sort out. Help us trust you—even when we don't know how things will work out. Thank you that you do not change and will be with us to take care of us . . . right now and tomorrow and forever. In Jesus's name, amen.

* Mark 10:15.

PSALM 137:1-6

¹ By the rivers of Babylon,

    we sat down and cried

    as we remembered Mount Zion;

² In the middle of Babylon,

    we hung up our harps on the poplar trees.

³ There, our slave masters

    tried to get us to sing songs.

Our enemies told us to be happy, saying,

    "Sing us one of those songs from Zion!"

⁴ But how can we sing the Lord's song

    when we are so far away from home?

⁵ If I forget you, Jerusalem,

    I hope my right hand also forgets how to play my

    harp.

⁶ My tongue might as well be glued to my mouth

    if I don't remember you,

if I don't say Jerusalem

    is my highest joy.

DAY 38

We Sat Down and Cried

Many years after David was king of Israel, many of the people began to follow bad kings who worshiped false gods. They started ignoring God's rules and hurting one another. They didn't listen when God told them to obey.

Because his people would not listen to him, God sent the Babylonians to capture them and take them out of Israel. People who had used to sing in God's temple on Mount Zion were dragged away to be slaves. The Babylonians forced them to make farms on dry and dusty land. It was very hard work.

Even worse, their slave-masters made fun of them. They would say, "You're supposed to be musicians! You should sing for us! Sing us one of those songs from Zion. Sing us a psalm about how Jerusalem can't be beaten because your God lives there. We want to laugh at your stupid song and your useless god." How could the people of Israel sing songs about how God would help them win, when God had let them be captured and taken so far away from their home and from him?

Would their songs be over forever? Should they give up and hang their harps on trees, like decorations instead of instruments? The temple in Jerusalem had meant everything to them. The only way they could sing again was if they were back home—and the only way they could go home would be if the Lord brought them back there again.

A psalm like this is hard for us to understand on days when we are happy and everything is going well. But some days the enemies of God's people seem to be winning. Some days they hurt us and make fun of us because we belong to God. On those days, this psalm makes more sense. Like the people who first sang it, we wonder if everything wrong will ever be made right. Will God make us happy again?

God tells us that he *will*—when he comes back to bring us home so that we can live with him. On that day, those who are happily hurting his people now will be punished. God will make us so happy that we will sing to him as loudly as we can, like those Israelites who sang their songs from Zion. Jesus will make everything better and happier than we can even imagine.

Heavenly Father, you sometimes call your people to go through very hard times. Sometimes those hard things happen because we ignore and disobey you. So we thank you that our Lord Jesus covers all our sins. Thank you that, because of him, you will not leave us far away from home forever but will bring us back to be with you. Thank you that one day we will all be together to sing happy songs of praise to you. Help us to be sorry for our sins, to ask you and really want you to forgive them, and to be hopeful because we can always count on your love and mercy. In Jesus's name, amen.

PSALM 139:1-12

¹ Lord, you have studied me, and you understand me
   completely.
² You know whenever I sit down and stand up.
   You know my thoughts before I think them.
³ You know when I get up and the times I stay in bed:
   You know all my habits very well.
⁴ Before a word comes out of my mouth,
   Lord, you know exactly what I'm going to say.
⁵ You are right behind me and right in front of me,
   and your hand covers me from above.
⁶ Your understanding of me is miraculous,
   at a level way too high for me to figure out.

[7] Where could I go to get away from you?
   Where could I run that you wouldn't already be?
[8] If I climb up to heaven, you're there;
   if I lie down in the lowest places on earth, you're
      there too.
[9] If I hide where the sun rises in the east,
   or go to live far beyond the sea to the west,
[10] even there your hand would lead me;
   your right hand would hold me tight.
[11] If I said, "I'm sure the darkness will hide me
   and the light will turn into night around me,"
[12] even darkness isn't dark to you,
   and night is as light as day:
   Darkness and light are all the same to you.

DAY 39

Where Could I Go to Get Away from You?

It's no fun for us to be on our own and not have anyone who understands us. Sometimes we are sad when we feel like no one knows what we think about, dream about, like, don't like, and even keep secret. But this psalm reminds us that *God* knows each of us completely. Nothing we can say or do surprises him—not even the things we do that surprise *us*! We can't go anywhere in the world to get away from God: Whether east or west, whether high or low, wherever we go, we will find that he is there before us. Even the pitch-black darkness can't hide us from God.

For those who hate God, that is a scary thought. God sees and knows all the bad things they think, say, and do. They can't hide anything from him. But for people who love God, this is wonderful news. We are glad that he is everywhere we go. That means he can protect us wherever we are. He is in front of us, behind us, and above us all the time. He knows when we try to do the right thing but make it come out all wrong. And he knows when we have sinned (again!)—so it is silly for us to pretend we didn't. We can quickly say sorry to him instead, and he will forgive us. Yes, God is with us no matter where we go. He watches over us even in the darkness.

When Jesus came to earth to save us, he knew that his Father was always with him too. He knew God went with him wherever he went. But when his enemies nailed him to a cross and the sky went dark, it seemed as if the Father *wasn't there* for him. He felt as though God had left him alone. Why was that? He had never done anything wrong. He had never pushed God away from him. He had always loved God. But he had taken the heavy weight of all *our* sin on top of him. He was dying to save us from that sin.

Even though Jesus felt as though God had left him alone, the Father was still with him in the darkness when he died. And even though Jesus felt as though God had left him alone, Jesus still trusted and loved God with his very last breath. The Father was happy with him and raised him from the dead. He lifted him up to the highest place in heaven. Now Jesus sits next to the Father and prays for us! Now, because of Jesus, God will always be with us to show us his love.

Lord of all creation, thank you that you fill this world. You are everywhere. We can never hide from you or be lost in a place where you can't find us. We can never surprise you. You know everything we will ever do, both good and bad, before we do it. That means we can never make you stop loving us because of something bad we did or thought. You will still love us because of Christ. Thank you that, because of him, you have forgiven us for all the bad things we do. We are *glad* you are always with us. Keep us close to you forever, Lord. Amen.

PSALM 150

¹ Praise the Lord!
Praise him in his holy temple;
    praise him in his majestic skies!
² Praise him for his powerful works;
    praise him for his supreme greatness!
³ Praise him with the sound of trumpets;
    praise him with harps and guitars!
⁴ Praise him with drums and dancing;
    praise him with violins and flutes!
⁵ Praise him with loud cymbals;
    praise him with crashing cymbals!
⁶ Everything that breathes, praise the Lord!
Praise the Lord!

Everything That Breathes, Praise the Lord!

Some parts of the Bible are hard to understand. This psalm is not one of those parts. *Everyone* can see that it's telling us to praise the Lord! Let the trumpets blast, and the orchestra go crazy, and the cymbals crash, and the flutes play loudly! Let all God's people show the joy in their hearts by dancing as they sing! Let the mighty angels in heaven's temple shout praises to the Lord! Let choirs sing and fill the skies with their music! Let birds and animals, dogs and cats, lions, tigers, and bears all join by barking, meowing, and roaring his praise. The Lord has made us and has saved us from our sins. He should be praised by every creature he has made. So praise the Lord!

(Oh, and you and I should join in too! Praise the Lord!)

Lord God, we want to join with all your creation and sing your praises today. You made the whole world out of nothing, and you rule over all things from your heavenly throne. The armies of angels in heaven sing your praises. The sun, moon, and stars sing your praises. The mountains and trees and animals and birds sing your praises. Lord, please let *us* join in their singing, even though we are such small and weak people, because we have the most to thank you for. You have not only made us but also rescued us: You've saved us from our sins and made us your children because of Christ. So we want to sing your praises too—and to have joyful shouts and wild celebrations because of you. Praise the Lord! Amen.

MORE CHRIST-CENTERED RESOURCES FOR FAMILIES

Books in the Pictures of Gospel Grace series retell lesser-known Bible stories to teach children how God shows his saving grace throughout his Word. Their chief aim is to direct children to the ultimate display of God's love and mercy to sinners—the redemption accomplished by the Lord Jesus Christ.

"There are never enough ways to convey the grace of God to children, and that's why I'm so excited about Pictures of Gospel Grace. This marvelous series is a great way to tell the story of God's favor and mercy over and over again to young readers!"
—Joni Eareckson Tada

ALSO BY IAIN M. DUGUID

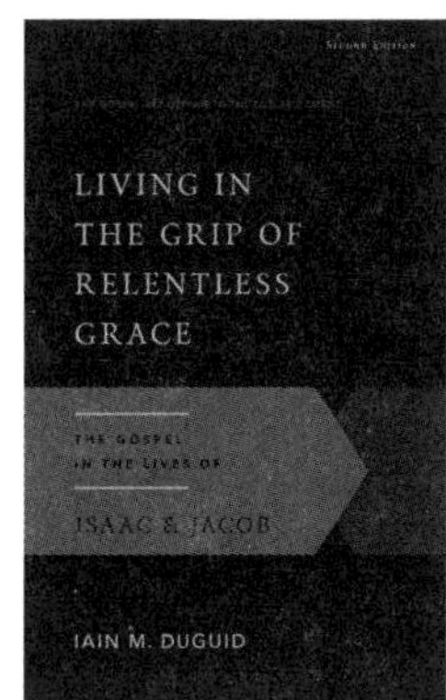

What do we do when God's promises seem to fall short of reality? In *Living in the Gap Between Promise and Reality*, Iain Duguid uses Abraham's story to point weary believers to the gospel, providing an example and profound encouragement for us today.

Isaac and Jacob's lives were sinful and messy—but God still used them. *Living in the Grip of Relentless Grace* shows us that the gospel is victorious through God's grace, not our flawed efforts.